About the Author

Memoirs of a Harrow Childhood is about my past life growing up in Harrow-on-the-Hill between 1943 and 1961 and my life as a daughter of a housemaster at Harrow School, a world-renowned boys' public school founded in 1572 and which now has satellite schools in such countries as Japan.

At the time I never questioned the privilege that came with the boarding school environment we grew up in, as for us at that time it was the only world we knew.

My reminiscences enabled me to capture in words a snapshot of life in a boarding school in the 1950s and include glimpses into the lives of some of my adventurous, intriguing and creative relatives from the Arctic explorer Neil Alison Mackintosh, who took part in the 1923 Antarctic Discovery expedition to well-respected artists like Alice Mackintosh (my grandmother).

Looking back through my memories led me to think about how life has changed to a world where time to enjoy simple pleasures has been buried under an avalanche of technology and constant noise.

Memoirs of a Harrow Childhood

Judith Davies

Memoirs of a Harrow Childhood

Vanguard Press

VANGUARD PAPERBACK

© Copyright 2024
Judith Davies

A CIP catalogue record for this title is
available from the British Library.

ISBN 978 1 80016 908 1

*Vanguard Press is an imprint of
Pegasus Elliot Mackenzie Publishers Ltd.*
www.pegasuspublishers.com

First Published in 2024

**Vanguard Press
Sheraton House Castle Park
Cambridge England**

Printed & Bound in Great Britain

Acknowledgements

This book could never have reached the public at all without the invaluable help of my friend, Myfanwy Cook, whose skill and encouragement have been immense.

FOREWORD

'In the beginning, was the nursery.'
Virginia Woolf.

History is the story of change, a lesson which every generation has to learn for itself.

As a child, I saw milk bottles made of glass being delivered from a heavy wooden cart pulled by a large shire horse with long hair hanging over its hoofs. My grandchildren bring it back from a supermarket in plastic containers. A way of life, and employment for both man and horse, not to mention harness makers, cart builders and glass workers, was swept away by this change.

What will disappear in my grandchildren's lifetime, for them to write about for their grandchildren?

Can there be many more useful things for our children to learn than that life was not always as they find it today? The dawning understanding of the changes wrought by history is of prime importance in education, and a thrilling journey of discovery for those who embark on it.

The sheer austerity of my childhood compared with that of children born in the twenty-first century is a big theme of this book. Materially speaking, we had much less. But intellectually and culturally, we had much more.

I don't remember having a new dress, as distinct from one "passed on" by somebody else, until I was eleven. I didn't have any say in its colour or design: it was checked Viyella with smocking on the bodice. I was pleased with it, although I didn't like the olive green and blue checks, simply because I was its first owner.

These details are clear in my memory more than fifty years later just because it was the first new dress of my life.

At five years old, our twin granddaughters made it clear everything, including boots, had to be pink or mauve.

We didn't have things their generation takes for granted: videos, teabags, computers, tracksuits, trainers or mobiles.

We weren't given choice. We were handed a plateful of food and expected to eat it. If we left the greens, we were exhorted to think of the poor little children with nothing to eat. It didn't occur to us to reject an item of clothing.

People did not, in the main, go in for wall-to-wall carpeting. Polished lino with one or two small rugs was typical in bedrooms; sometimes there were just bare boards. These were cold in winter and full of splinters.

Homes were not heated to the temperature they are today. Central heating was by no means universal.

People did not expect a single T-shirt to be adequate wear all through the winter.

It followed from that that people wore much more in winter than they do today. Our outlines were distorted by layer after layer to be adequately clad. The miniskirt would have been an impossibility.

If my grandchildren read this, they will see that just as our lives in the 1940s and 1950s were so different from theirs in 2023, so will their children's, and grandchildren's, be from their own.

One chapter of this book, in expanded form, was part of a talk I gave entitled, "How I became an Art Teacher" to the University of the Third Age in Tavistock, Devon in September 2004. Thank you to that group, whose need for a talk set me thinking.

The main impetus to writing it, however, came from my task, as executor, of clearing the flat that Joanna, my elder sister, had rented for twenty-seven years until her death in 2003.

The extraordinarily rich hoard of papers, documents, references, house particulars, photograph albums, letters, scrapbooks and notebooks which I uncovered there were the history of the family in tangible form. There was also a great deal about the family's relationship with Harrow School, whose ethos dominated our lives.

When I looked at the large number of letters preserved right down to the envelopes in which they'd been sent, it seemed wrong and a waste to simply tip them into a black plastic sack. The history of our family was in them.

So, what at first sight seemed a completely impossible task of sorting, identifying, categorising and (in many cases) disposing of a sea of paper became something quite different. The sadness of dealing with the material possessions of one who had died was transformed by the reading of many documents which shed light on the lives of people in my family.

From the rich treasure trove unearthed, I began to form a belief that I should make a memoir of my early life. The several people who made up my world to the age of eleven deserved commemoration. The physical beauty of that world, although affected by the scars left by the Second World War, contained many green fields now obliterated by housing.

I needed to put down on paper the memories of these people, and some unspoilt places, before a time arrived when I could no longer remember them. If I delayed doing it any longer, Alzheimers might set in, and the past would be lost.

CHAPTER 1 – INTRODUCTION

I was born at Roxeth Mead, a Georgian house on the western slopes of Harrow-on-the-Hill, in 1943. The house had a veranda and broad lawns. Next door, there was a large orchard belonging to the house of a friend of my father's. This almost rural setting was also the scene of my first school. In another part of the building was the small school I attended from the age of four til eleven.

We lived at Roxeth Mead from 1943 to 1946. We then moved up to the top of the hill, when my father, newly returned from the war, was made housemaster at Bradbys. This meant he was now in charge of fifty boys who boarded at Bradbys. It was a larger, Victorian house, built in 1848, of which my clearest early memory is being given a scooter to play on. My elder sister, Joanna, had a "fairy cycle" — the two-wheeler to which you progressed after having a tricycle.

Three months after we moved, my younger sister, Gillian, was born. The nurse assisting my mother came into my room in the early morning and announced that I now had a baby sister.

This was quite a surprise, as I had no idea any such event was in the offing. But I accepted it philosophically and, after a while, the dark, curly-haired Gillian, was ready to join in our games of tea parties, schools and mothers and fathers.

Gillian, with her black eyebrows and eyelashes, so different from the fairer colouring of the rest of the family, was supposed to be a throwback to an earlier generation.

Although the winter of 1946-47, when she was born, was one of the coldest on record, it was still believed to be correct to put the baby out in her pram no matter how low the temperature was.

At four and a half, I was sent to the small school which occupied half of Roxeth Mead. We could not, in my parents' view, be sent to a state school, because if we had been, we would have had to mix with people they regarded as "gutter snipes". At that period of history, no one in our family had ever been sent to any school except a fee-paying one.

So, my parents went without many things they would have liked, to afford to send us to independent schools.

Roxeth Mead was run, with confident eccentricity, by a Froëbel-trained teacher, Miss Nicholson, universally referred to as "Miss Nick".

On my first day, I was led into a classroom where children older than I were chanting words written on the blackboard. I was immediately convinced that reading was utterly beyond me and I would never master it.

Evidently, this view was unnecessarily pessimistic.

There were boys in the school up to the age of eight or nine, when they were generally sent to boarding schools. Girls stayed until eleven, but there was one famous girl who stayed on until she was sixteen, and became a greeting card designer.

My mother suffered from a frustrated wish to send us to her Scottish boarding school. But the cost, for three of us, plus all the travelling and uniform costs, was far beyond what my parents could afford. I was eternally grateful not to have been sent away to a school where I am certain non-conformists would not have been welcome. I was also suspicious of the emphasis on sporting prowess that boarding schools seemed to have.

I can't remember being bullied at the first of my two schools, but we did cruelly gang up on a half-Russian girl who came to the school whose differentness (refugee, beautiful) aroused our animosity.

Miss Nick, unusually, confided in the children over one aspect of the report inspectors made about the school, "Not enough lavatories", she announced. There was one. When one wanted to visit the loo, one had to raise a hand and say, "May I be excused please?" For years afterwards, being excused from anything aroused in my mind a vision of that rather cold, square little room with coconut matting.

We were taught more than just the three Rs. Latin and French also featured. On sports day, there was every kind of race: egg and spoon, sack, three-legged and little-brothers-and-sisters. Clumsy and uncoordinated as I was, I never won anything. However, our headmistress had one very advanced idea; every child who had taken part got a prize, whether they'd come first or last.

This anti-elitist stance was at odds with the prevailing idea, which was that only the best got recognition.

Her belief that we would be damaged by having experienced failure seems to me now infinitely touching and generous. A different lesson could have been learned from failure; that we were not all good at everything, but of course, there were other ways we could learn this.

There were other intriguing customs. If our birthdays fell on a school day, we were allowed to choose the hymn sung at prayers that morning. This was regarded as a great honour. I invariably chose "Blest are the pure in heart", because its rather facile tune appealed to me. I made no connection with its origin in The Beatitudes.

At prayers, Miss Nick, a small figure in a tweed suit, played the piano vigorously.

She was given to deploring our behaviour and saying how much worse it was than that of the children who'd left before we arrived at the school.

It was expected that we would become proficient at mental arithmetic. Without computers or calculators, our brains had to perform the functions of these machines. Wrongly spelt words had to be written out ten times correctly. This tedious practice enabled us to spell with confidence.

On Monday afternoons, it was dancing. A teacher came out from London to teach this. At first, I was very attracted to dancing but had no sense of rhythm or the accurate movements demanded in the ballet lessons which followed our dancing ones. Eventually, I realised that what drew me to both ballet and more general dancing was the sound of the music.

On Friday afternoons, it was painting. Another special teacher, dressed exotically, came to do art with us. I looked forward all week to this session. When I was nine, she suggested I started doing oil painting. This big adventure was the despair of my mother because I got the paint all over my clothes. But it was very, very exciting learning to do it.

Was it an adequate primary education? Was it, in any way, a preparation for life? Based as it was, on three great pillars of English culture; the King James Bible, the English Hymnal, and some of Shakespeare's plays, I believe it was.

But in worldly terms, it was inadequate. While at this school, I took and failed the exam known as the Eleven-plus. I knew my maths was poor and slow, and we had never heard of, let alone studied, the subject known as Verbal Reasoning, but were still expected to be able to cope with this in the exam. Our somewhat untypical curriculum had included Legends of Greece and Rome, but not the skills we needed to pass this exam, the passing of which determined whether one had a free place at the secondary school, of our parents' choice.

In this present age of the National Curriculum, I suppose this could not happen now. Science and computing must be learned, and our early contact with language and arts-based subjects would not happen now, or not in the same way.

However, those years from four to eleven in a very small school with virtually no facilities left me with a lasting love of literature, music and painting. Did this come from home or school, or from a combination I was fortunate to experience?

I also made a friendship at that school which has lasted all my life. My elder sister made two friendships which were very important to her, and one of these was lifelong. My younger sister also made a friendship there which has endured half a century.

If school is not about instilling a love for the fruits of civilisation, then I do not know what it is about. These friendships were a bonus which supported us through some of the difficulties which lay ahead of us.

In our childhood, we had one great blessing. We were free from the tyranny of the mobile phone and independent of all other electronic gadgets. We did not feel the compulsion to listen to pop music in all circumstances including country walks and bus and train journeys.

We listened instead to the sounds of nature; the same ones Shakespeare and Keats had heard, birdsong, wind and water and animals lowing.

In our London suburbs, we did sometimes hear aeroplanes. From the top of Harrow-on-the-Hill, you could just see planes coming in to land at Heathrow. But they were less frequent than today, and the curse of rowdy aviation did not blight the whole of West London, as it does now.

The noise of car and lorry traffic in central London could be heard as a distant hum ten miles away in Harrow.

Another sound we often heard was when a man driving a horse and cart used to shout, "Rag and bone." He collected all sorts of unwanted items, an early precursor of the great efforts at recycling which go on today.

CHAPTER 2 – MY FATHER

My father, John Wade Thompson, was born on 1st January 1908. Because of the date, he was never known by any other Christian name than Jan.

He was the son of Arthur Ralph Thompson, a consultant urologist at Guy's Hospital in London, and his wife, Florence, née Wansey. He was the eldest of four siblings and the elder of two brothers. At the time of his birth, his parents lived at 4 St. Thomas Street, Southwark.

He went first to Montpelier School, Paignton, and then to Brighton College, Sussex. After that, he did his degree at Pembroke College, Cambridge.

For reasons I have been unable to discover, the costs of his education and that of his siblings were paid for by a benevolent uncle. Possibly this was because Ralph and Florence Thompson separated, and two establishments had to be maintained.

At Cambridge, he was recommended to read geography, instead of maths, his first choice. He then went to teach, first in Belfast and then at Monmouth School.

While employed at Monmouth, my father assembled a large collection of durable, fabric-backed maps of all the areas within hailing distance of that border town; coastal Somerset, the Vale of the Severn, and the Forest of Dean. Evidently, he hoped to explore these in detail, with their rich variety of geographical features, famous ruins and peerless landscape. But in January 1933, he was appointed to the post of Assistant Master at Harrow, so the maps were put aside, perhaps for future holidays, and his bags packed to work in the London commuter belt.

He remained at Harrow until 1966 when a catastrophic stroke ended his career. During the Second World War, he was called up into the King's Royal Rifle Corps and was absent for some time from Harrow, training officers. He came back from war service a Major and was known by that title for years afterwards.

The Governors of Harrow School, his peacetime employers, applied to the War Office for my father to be demobbed in 1944, in order to re-open one of the boys' houses at Harrow, which had been closed during the war. They also stated that they required his services to make up the teaching complement of the school.

His Army Record Office papers show that A.P. Boissier, the Head Master of the day, stated, "the post for which Mr Thompson is required is one that requires particular knowledge and experience and could not adequately be filled by a substitute."

After one broken engagement, he met my mother at a wedding of mutual friends in London in 1938. He was an usher and she a bridesmaid. They were married on 1st April 1939. Three children were born to them: Joanna in 1940; I in 1943 and Gillian at the end of 1946.

My earliest conscious memory of my father was of trying to keep up with his long, brisk military strides. Holding his hand, I used to run to keep up. I implored him several times on each outing to slow down so I could keep up, but each time the pace returned to its original one.

He was six feet two inches tall and strongly-built. The army had made him stand with good posture, as with so many of his contemporaries. I never knew him without glasses. He smoked a pipe, like many men of his generation. He was interested in all sports and had played rugby for his college.

We learned his tastes as children. His favourite book was "The Riddle of the Sands". His favourite music was the New World Symphony, followed by Gilbert and Sullivan operettas.

Having read geography, he had an extraordinarily detailed knowledge of the lie of the land in numerous English counties. I used to be astonished when we were driving a long distance to a holiday, to see the way he drove without maps. Only when we reached some nest of lanes in the furthest outposts of the Celtic fringe would the well-thumbed fabric maps appear, after which he unerringly reached the destination.

Being his children, we first had to learn to read, then to read maps. Once Joanna had mastered this art, I had to.

His enjoyment of the different landscapes of Britain and abroad was communicated to us very early on. He gave us a thorough grounding in the climate and geology of our native land, and the reasons for each area's differentness from the others.

He was certain we should know something of contemporary drama and fiction. He took us to the startlingly innovative "Waiting for Godot" and, most memorably, read "On the Beach" by Neville Shute. This novel was a devastating prediction of the end of mankind after a nuclear holocaust. His instruction to me to read this reappears later in this book as a force which shaped me.

When I first remember him, he was about forty, doing his job as housemaster. This work carried perhaps a certain status, but a low salary. Living accommodation was free because one lived on the premises where one's work was done, but the responsibility was huge. Being in loco parentis for fifty boys, managing the live-in domestic staff and his own family, as well as teaching in the classroom was a role I have since come to realise was a full life. Just to take the number and range of interactions with other people in the course of a single day is to realise what energy, what grasp of the detail and what firmness of purpose were required.

Housemasters were expected to move straight from being assistant masters to being experts in adolescent psychology, personnel officers and something of a hotel manager. Contacts with preparatory schools had to be maintained, in order that their headmasters would send their boys to Harrow. We attended many a preparatory school cricket match or speech day.

In the house, all the furnishings of the boys' rooms, and all the boys' food and laundry had to be provided out of not-very-generous funds.

Part of his job was having to do difficult things, like breaking the news to a boy in his house of the boy's father's death. That particular boy's father had had severe war wounds in the Second World War, and he had, after years of pain, died from them in his late thirtiess.

My father also had to "do" confirmation classes. This entailed reminding candidates for confirmation of what Christianity was about so that they could become fully participating members of the Church of England. No training for this was given or expected. Housemasters were simply presumed able to do it.

Relaxation, when it was possible, which was not often until the school holidays, was golf. This was played with three colleagues, at Sandy Lodge, near Rickmansworth. Indigent school masters were given a special rate to enable them to afford — just — to do this.

Much later, when retired and disabled, gardening became a consuming passion. From his mother, he had inherited the love of growing things. His vegetable garden in Cambridge, lush at summer's end with giant groves of runner beans and immense parsnips, was all cultivated with one hand. The other was useless after his stroke. He limped between the apple and pear trees, their leaves glossy with health and their branches weighed down with fruit, laboriously cultivating a free supply of vegetables.

With the same refusal to be beaten by his disability, he had taught himself to write with his left hand.

He had a habit which I noticed from an early age. Each morning, he had a clean strip of paper on his desk on which he wrote down all the tasks he had to do and all the things he must not forget that day. As each item was accomplished, he crossed it off. No one else but himself could have read his dashing script, but it was crystal clear to him. I found myself doing likewise. He was orderly and methodical. His desk was always tidy. Unfortunately, I did not inherit this trait.

Back in the 1950s, we began to understand that my father, while determined to introduce us to some contemporary fiction and drama, was also devoted to some classic authors. He liked Scott — an author hardly ever read nowadays — especially "Marmion". Perhaps I was only taken to the film "Ivanhoe" because my father believed it would be a worthy one. Perhaps significantly, the only scene from the film, which I can remember more than sixty years after seeing it, is the wedding. Mediaeval jousts, sieges, crusades and witchcraft vanished from my recall.

All through his adult life, my father was a Freemason. Through this organisation, with its countrywide network of groups, he met people with whom he made lasting friendships. The charitable work performed by Masonic Chapters made it a worthy club. The secrecy attached to all aspects of its operation made us curious. I don't think he ever got any career advantage out of this. He evidently enjoyed the all-male society, in spite of having it when he was a boy at school, university and work. Its main benefit for him was that he made life-long friendships at his Lodges.

Perhaps the need for male companionship in his middle years arose from being surrounded by four women at home. Perhaps he yearned for conversation that only men could have with him. Perhaps after the kind of education he'd had, he only felt truly relaxed in the company of other men. He also met at meetings men who were not schoolmasters, which must have been important.

My father's study in Bradbys had one door into it from our side of the house, and one from the boys' side of it. Here was where he was often to be found.

It had a red Turkey carpet and white shelves of books in the alcoves. There was a big leather-covered Edwardian desk, with drawers down each side of the kneehole.

On the walls were several frames each containing sixteen or twenty "leaving photographs". These were ordered from the school photographer when any boy left the school and presented to masters who had known them.

They were reminders to him of the many boys who had been in his care. Perhaps, because he was the father of three daughters, some of them were substitute sons. These, the ones he'd liked, maintained contact with him long after they'd left the school. They asked my parents to their weddings and christenings — sometimes to their second weddings as well. Perhaps, to some of them, he was a surrogate father, a male role model for those who lacked this in their own family.

Manners and etiquette mattered to my parents. My father complained because I had not been introduced to a boy of eighteen whom I met at a dance when I was sixteen, and was proposing to go out with him. People must have been introduced.

Was he unrealistic in expecting me, in 1960, to share this view?

I think he was. He hankered after the standards which he believed had prevailed "pre-war".

I was too immature to ask, as I might have done, whether introduction was a guarantee of probity or any other value. Clearly, from the literature, ne'er-do-wells, black sheep, bounders and cads had existed from the dawn of history. Since no introduction had taken place, my father contented himself with phoning the ex-headmaster of my friend, who was a neighbour of ours, to ask if my friend was "all right". Luckily, he was.

By the time I was a teenager, I believed that my parents embodied everything that was old-fashioned and out-of-date. I no longer regarded them as omniscient. Their politics were incomprehensible to me. In these regards, no doubt I resembled most of my peers. It took me decades to realise and acknowledge that their values and priorities were mainly sound.

When he retired from being a housemaster and became an ordinary master instead, he took on the voluntary job of being a Church Warden at St. Mary's. This is a role which involves much responsibility and many tedious hours counting collections and seeing that all is ready for services. Christian convictions and a strong urge to do something for the community, of which he'd been a member by then for thirty years, came together in this job. It was quite a heavy extra duty for one still employed as a teacher — or as he had always wished to be known, a schoolmaster.

He was a very modest man. He'd done so many things he'd never told us about. Only a third at Cambridge, but boxed for the university and played rugby for his college. His boxing medal carefully kept in its presentation box was acquired for the performance of what has become a very unfashionable sport today.

He'd canoed down the Moselle in the 1930s. He'd trained officers in the war. He'd survived growing up in what is known as a broken home. He became the only one of four siblings to get married, stay married and have a family.

He'd seen the dangerous world of southeast England of 1940 and feared for the family's safety. Then he'd seen what he regarded as a degenerate 1960s world and wondered what had happened to pre-war standards. He deplored the "cult of personality".

He didn't have the sons perhaps he'd hoped for. The balance of the sexes in our family was only corrected in the next generation when three sons were born to me and my husband. He grew up with the demographic imbalance caused by the First World War. Men only ten years older than him had been slaughtered in the trenches.

He made strenuous efforts to civilise boys who were boorish, oafish, thick or rebellious. It wore him out. "Any fool can teach clever boys," he'd said.

He'd been a big family man, doing his best to support and advise two single sisters. He'd put other people first: his charges in the schools where he'd worked, his wife and children and the community in Harrow-on-the-Hill.

It is impossible ever to listen to the cor anglais solo in the New World Symphony without feeling a direct link between myself and my father. Homesickness, famously portrayed in that piece, may have been as familiar to my father as to Dvorak.

Every term at Harrow a 'Field Day' was held, when the corps, a group of boys who did services training one

31

afternoon a week, left the school premises to go on exercises.

Some boys were not due to take part in any form of military activity that day and my father was tasked with finding them occupations. He drove them into the nearby countryside, several miles from the school, selected the most sensible boy present to be in charge of the group, and said, "Now find your way back to Harrow."

It would in the twenty-first century be impossible to issue, let alone follow, such an instruction. Risk assessments would prevent it. And yet that expedition must have fostered the growth of initiative and a spirit of co-operation.

Presumably, they all did get back to Harrow safely. Perhaps someone will read this who was a member of that party.

CHAPTER 3 – MY MOTHER

My mother was born Helen Mackintosh, the fifth and last child of John Stewart Mackintosh, a physician, and Alice, born Ballard, his wife.

In her childhood, as in mine, the two-parent family was the norm, except where spouses had been bereaved by war or other untimely death. In her childhood families of five or six were not at all unusual; in mine, that number was becoming rare. Many families we knew had 2 or 3 children.

Family size continued to shrink in the last part of the twentieth century, one point eight children per family became the average.

She was by some years the youngest, and my grandparents had to lay down ground rules that her three much older brothers were not to tease her.

My grandmother, her mother, who lived to be ninety-three, had great talent as a portrait painter. She produced portraits of all her children, and of others. The cheapness of servants meant that her nursery, occupied for many years by the five children, was staffed generously, and this freed her to develop her talent.

The portrait of my mother, aged five, and standing in the garden between Madonna lilies as tall as herself, and wearing a white dress with a blue stain sash, is a classic. With hair flowing down her back, my mother's rapt innocence radiantly conveys the Wordsworthian view of childhood.

The garden in which she stands in the painting belonged to Corner House, the house on the corner of Platts Lane and Finchley Road, which stood there until the site was bought by Westfield College in the fifties. That was her home until she was sent to boarding school at St. Andrew's in Scotland, at thirteen in 1923.

After leaving school, she did secretarial training and worked in London, living independently in flats, until marrying my father in 1939.

My mother's tastes were vehemently held and expressed.

Such was her influence on mine that, following her insistence that all three of the houses she lived in during my lifetime, must have a duck-egg blue drawing room, I found myself certain that the room we sat in after Hugh and I were married must also be that colour.

Of course, you could say that influence didn't come into it; it was just a colour which we both liked. But the pale blue environment of my early life, the peonies in a glass vase and the polished dining table, all reappeared decades later in my married days.

However, I never felt any urge to reproduce the pea green and white striped paper which lined our dining room at Bradbys.

My mother would relate how despised William Morris's designs had been in the days of her youth. In the 1960s, he was rediscovered, and it was once again chic to have your walls and windows covered with paper and fabric from those designs. The cyclical nature of fashion, later spelt out to me by a lecture James Laver gave at Harrow, took root in my mind.

I was fascinated by various aspects of her femininity.

In my parents' bedroom, there was a white-painted bedroom suite from Maples. Her dressing-table, white with a glass top, had little drawers full of bottles and lipsticks. In a larger drawer were handkerchiefs in sweet pea colours. These handkerchiefs, so small and flimsy, some of silk and others very fine lawn, were hardly functional. Some, treasured by my sister, Joanna, after my mother had died, were in fragments when I discovered them in 2003.

They were relics of an age before the paper tissue took over. If you were a lady, you always had one with you.

I would watch her painting her nails with mid-pink polish and wish I could do the same.

She had hair almost down to her waist so washing and drying it was a major operation. She kept for the rest of her life, the hairstyle she'd adopted after 1945. A thick lock of hair was rolled up on either side of her forehead. These were secured with hairpins, and the rest was worn in a bun at the back of her neck. In 1950, this was fashionable, and a copy of Vogue in my possession shows this, on the cover, to be so. I don't think she ever saw a hairdresser between 1939 and her death in 1984.

She brushed this hair with ivory-backed brushes and looked at her reflection in a hand mirror made of the same material. In the 1930s when she acquired these objects, no one protested that killing elephants for their tusks was cruel. Lots of things were made of ivory and it was accepted that this was a normal thing to do.

By the same token, fur coats were regarded with envy by those who could not afford one. They were looked upon as a definite status symbol. Animal rights activists had not been born.

My mother exercised great restraint about what she would allow herself to wear. The only time I ever saw her use eye makeup was at my wedding.

Her views about clothes were prim. One must never look cheap, vulgar, loud or fast. Nothing revealing, no clashing colours, no tight skirts or trousers and no ladders or wiggly seams in stockings.

She never possessed a washing machine. Sheets and pillowcases went to the laundry, a business where industrial-sized washing machines washed and dried the bedclothes of hundreds of people, and then delivered them back clean. Often, the wrong ones were sent back, necessitating lengthy complaints to the management.

Everything else she washed by hand, pumping everything vigorously up and down in a cloud of detergent bubbles, wringing it over the sink and then hanging it all out in the open to dry. When we were babies in nappies, and before the invention of plastic pants, the amount of washing must have been phenomenal. There were no disposables of anything; handkerchiefs had to be boiled in an old saucepan and nappies soaked and washed daily.

My mother greatly disliked ironing, so a woman who was paid eight old pence an hour (about 3p in 2006 money), the going rate in the 1950s, came in on a Tuesday afternoon to do it for her.

Miss Long was her name. She would put down the iron on its special asbestos-lined plate to talk, and one had to be careful not to bring up too many topics. Like many of her generation, she was utterly devoted to the family for whom she worked, and turned up faithfully for many years.

But they remained "Mrs Thompson" and "Miss Long" throughout this long friendship. The barriers between classes had to be maintained.

When I became a teenager, my half-term treat was a trip up to London with my mother. This meant lunch out, a sandwich and a cake in a coffee bar and a look at clothes in big department stores. Each autumn, she believed I needed a new party dress. These were always in shiny fabrics with a close-fitting bodice and gathered skirt and needed big petticoats.

In her favourite store, Marshall and Snelgrove, she lingered longingly by the clothes for her age group.

She went without things for herself that she would have liked in order for us to be seen at our best. She dutifully bought us good warm tweed coats for winter, for which we were not grateful enough. Once, she lent me a dress I rather coveted of hers to go out with the boyfriend of the moment. It was made of the new miracle fabric terylene.

She went in a lot for mending things which had gone into holes. During the Second World War, everyone had to do this as you just could not get replacements. In the 50s and 60s, there were plenty in the shops, but I think the habit of mending things had stuck, and she also probably felt she could not spend that amount of money on herself. Her special winter vests and knickers had dozens of very neat darns so that they would go on lasting a little longer.

Indeed, mending things was very highly thought of by another member of my family, Aunt Jessie. She declared that some of her moments of greatest satisfaction and fulfilment had been while darning curtains. These darns were exquisite works of art, with exact matching of thread to the background.

She was a very good needlewoman and knitter when we were infants, making all our dresses and jackets.

She felt some envy for another master's wife, who was known to have what were called "private means".

This woman always appeared in the latest fashion on formal school occasions. I remember her trapeze-line dress worn at the annual Eton v. Harrow cricket march at Lords. A blurry blue print, it billowed out from her slim shoulders, a nine-day wonder. "Don't stare," mother said to us, sotto voce.

Later, this same master's wife had a nose job. It was very unusual then to have plastic surgery for aesthetic reasons. When my mother saw the result, she sighed and said it must be nice to be able to afford that sort of thing.

When I became old enough to be aware of my mother's health, she was never well. Diverticulitis gave her a lot of pain. Smoking from the age of seventeen, she was unable to give up cigarettes and coughed. Her skin wrinkled early and her ankles were swollen. Arthritis afflicted her hand and her rings had to be enlarged. Because of all these troubles she had less stamina than some.

When the great definition of class membership was said to be that you were either U or non-U, my mother eagerly took it up. She made sure that she said, "looking glass" not "mirror", "notepaper" rather than "writing paper" and looked down on people who said "lounge" instead of "drawing room" or "sitting room". Above all, one must not say "perfume", it had to be "scent". She also said you had to be very suspicious of people who were seen to have new luggage as it signalled that you were nouveau riche. Of course, a lot of the parents of boys at Harrow came into this category, which enabled her to feel superior.

After discovering what death was, in the bodies of baby birds who had fallen from their nests or been caught by the cats, I asked my mother about it; were we really all going to die? And what would I do when she died?

"It's all right," she said. "I won't die for ages, and when I do, you'll have a family of your own to love." Prophetic words: it was exactly as she said it would be. But that didn't stop her death, when it came, being a massive loss. When she died, I hadn't thanked her for all her labour on my behalf, or her love.

As a small girl, I could not envisage a world in which she was not present, playing a big part. And yet, I accepted what she said because I regarded her, at that era of my life, as being an authority.

Later, my thoughts returned to the question: "If I'm going to die, how can the world carry on existing and being, without me in it?" I never articulated this thought to any grown-up; perhaps I was afraid of seeming stupid by asking it.

Birth was another mystery. I was not intimate enough with my mother to ask how could the baby not be there at one moment, but be there, a separate being, the next. It was never explained to me, before reading our biology textbook at secondary school, how this happened. I was never brave enough to ask my mother, having picked up vibrations that this was somehow a topic that grown-ups did not want to talk about. I lacked the confidence to ask.

But although I did not receive that form of enlightenment, there were many positive influences. My mother had a wooden box of cotton reels, darning wool and needles, which were frequently used to repair our clothes. On the lid was pasted a sepia photograph of a lake in winter, the water dark and icy-looking. There were snow-covered verges and trees hanging over it, their filigree twigs white with frost.

Underneath the picture, it said, "If winter comes, can spring be far behind?" My mother was greatly attached to this quotation, as she responded to anything to do with the weather and the seasons.

I didn't know at that time that it was from Shelley's "Ode to the West Wind". How strange that I should first meet a line from that work on a box of mending equipment.

Her reaction to changes in weather was always dramatic. If a summer day reached 80°f, she would declare, "This heat makes me feel quite ill."

She had, in the late 1950s, £25 a month with which to clothe herself and three daughters. I remember a sense of guilt when I had to have a new pair of what were called "walking shoes". The amount of walking involved in each journey to and from school meant heavy expenditure on shoes. They cost a whole £4.

It was a heroic effort to manage on so little money. One has to admire what she achieved.

Her early experiences and enthusiasms were so important to her that one of them at any rate was transmitted to me.

As a small child, my mother had been taken for holidays from London, to a farm at The Lee, Buckinghamshire. This was then seen as remote from London. Now, of course, people commute to and from The Lee. It is a haunt of the wealthy, with large houses and gardens.

In those days, it was a dusty journey into the middle of the Chilterns. The landscape around the farm was the first one my mother learned to love. There, she found a lost paradise.

Later on in her life, she experienced a multitude of other very different ones: Scotland, where she went to boarding school; South Africa and Rhodesia (as it then was); Switzerland, where she went skiing; Dorset, Suffolk, and France, where we had holidays.

But that early attachment to the woods, fields and lanes around The Lee made her into a lifelong conservationist. Of all her legacies to me, that was the most important. Others mattered too (mending things, carefulness with money, the family), but that is the one I value most.

The next most important thing she did for me was to take me, once, to the ballet, when I was nine. It was "The Sleeping Beauty".

From the first darkening of the auditorium and notes of music, I was transported to a world of dreams:

colour, music and an immortal fairy story. My immediate discovery, that the characters did not speak but had to act, was reported to her in a loud whisper.

Gwen Raverat, describing her 1890s childhood in the 1980s, says that when the family visited London relations, men of the underclass would run all the way from King's Cross to Kensington Square in order to earn a tip by carrying luggage upstairs.

In my mother's and aunt's childhood, between 1910 and 1920, the same thing happened. Men ran behind the cab from London termini to Platts Lane in order to unload the luggage and earn a tip.

So, nothing improved, in the situation of London's poor, between 1890 and 1920.

These occasional glimpses, in my mother's childhood, of the existence of the have-nots, did not turn her into a socialist. In her early adult life, unemployment was at catastrophic levels. She acquired, and serenely maintained, Conservative convictions. She distrusted socialists, with the single exception of Ernest Bevin, whom she admired.

She was extremely interested in the weather. Perhaps that made her typically British. She never missed the weather forecast on the radio. Other aspects of the natural world cropped up regularly in her conversation. If one heard birds singing at an untimely stage of the winter, perhaps on a sunny day, she would say, "poor things — they think it's spring".

When the cat caught a bird, doomed by its youth and injuries to die, she felt a severe conflict of loyalty. She was devoted to the cat but wracked by pity for the bird.

Some of her pronouncements were very green. Stuck behind some immense lorry load of something bulky, she would demand, "Why on earth don't they send it by train?"

She mistrusted educated women — except possibly the teachers at my secondary school. Graduate wives were still in a small minority in my childhood, and she looked upon them with suspicion. Another prejudice was Americans, who in her view, imported their alien culture, which she regarded as debased. Never having read much American literature or looked at paintings or architecture from that country, enabled her to go on feeling superior.

In the period which lay after the time covered by this account (1943-59) my mother faced the biggest difficulties of her life. My father had a disabling stroke in 1966. Overnight, he changed from being a senior master employed at Harrow, to a speechless and paralysed invalid. Some of his movement and speech returned haltingly, after many efforts both by him and by speech and physiotherapists. But there had been considerable brain damage.

My mother had to become responsible for everything. She had to care for a husband who could not express himself and whose frustration affected them

44

both. The cruelty of this blow, shortly before my father was due to retire, struck everyone who knew them.

For nine years, my mother cared for him and organised everything. Then he died of a heart attack. At sixty-five she had to cope with being a widow.

In all this, she was called upon to display the same fortitude as her generation had all had to find within themselves during the war.

She also had to confront the immense difficulties created by the mental state of my elder sister. She had years of grief over Joanna's unhappiness, her many illnesses and her difficulties with employment and employers. The torment of this illness affected both of them.

She'd been a devoted daughter and a loving mother to three daughters. I failed to show her my gratitude when I should have done but realise, too late, my debt to her.

CHAPTER 4 – THE SERVANTS

To maintain a house which contained fifty boys, five family members and the living-in staff, it was necessary to employ help.

Managing the servants had been a big middle-class preoccupation in Georgian, Victorian and Edwardian times. Relationships with those on whose toil life in Bradbys depended were a time-consuming part of my parents' lives.

There was a shifting population of maids recruited from the West of Ireland. One of them, Bridie, stayed with us for years, loyally supporting us. Others came and went.

One of them, Esther, got so paralytically drunk on her evening out once that my mother had to carry her up four flights of stairs to bed to sleep it off. It may well have happened more than once and had become a regular part of life.

Another, Mary, was found one day in a psychotic state, denouncing the people who did nothing to stop the Irish Famine, which by the time of which I write had been over for one hundred years. That didn't make it any the less dreadful for those who suffered in it, of course. She had to be taken away to an asylum not far off, where many of Greater London's sectioned psychiatric cases were treated in those days.

We also had on the staff a man whose title was "butler". In fact, I think a lot of his time was spent stoking the boiler in the basement. The efficient operation of this device was the reason why I never, from the age of three til we left the house the year I was seventeen, ever felt cold indoors. From heavy, cast iron radiators, a magnificent heat poured forth.

There were two cooks, one self-taught called Mrs Butt, my mother's most loyal defender. The other, Miss Barker, was college-trained in the modern manner. She eventually married one of the school's gardening staff and moved away. From her, I learned my first ever dish, gingerbread, which I used to make in her kitchen on Saturday afternoons.

These people worked, uncomplainingly as far as I knew, in a dark basement below street level. Lights had to be on all day in the four larders with slate shelves and windows made of metal with punched holes in them. A corridor with several corners led to the pantry where Bridie washed our china, the scullery where the vegetables were prepared, and the boiler room. Daily Bridie cut thin bread and butter and carried a large tray laden with china up the stairs from the basement to the dining room, before ringing a Swiss cowbell which called us to tea.

I was not, at the time it happened, allowed to know anything about the drunkenness of Esther. Unexpected hazards of this sort were only one of the ways in which my parents had a bit more to contend with than they expected when they took on the care of fifty boys.

The staff ate their meals in a staff dining room, which was also in the basement but which, because of the slope of the hill, looked out onto the garden.

So, we had an "upstairs" life and a glimpse of a "below stairs" one. To my shame, when I went to the west of Ireland three years after leaving Bradbys, I did not visit Bridie in her home town, near which I had a holiday job. Was it shyness or snobbery? I was a stranger in a strange land; she was among her own people. I was also an intruder and representative of a nation which had almost destroyed hers. What tales she might have told me if I'd had the grace to visit her.

In contrast with that so-distant era, I have never once, in forty years of marriage, ever employed anyone to clean, cook or sew in our house. But then, I've never had fifty boys to look after.

It seemed entirely normal to us that boys called our father "Sir". The complex hierarchy of the boys' life in school, was echoed in the customs of life below stairs. Our two cooks were addressed by Mrs or Miss and their surnames; the maids were known only by their Christian names.

The people working below stairs had very little in the way of mechanisation. I remember the daily rumble

FROM EILEEN TESSA HAWKES
TO SUE RICHES
07578805022

of a primitive potato peeling machine. I recall there were Hoovers for large areas and even a domestic floor polisher. Other than that, it was a laborious round of laying and clearing tables, sweeping floors and corridors, polishing wooden surfaces, cleaning showers, bathrooms and lavatories and cleaning the boys' small cell-like rooms.

With dusters and dustpans, with feather dusters and floor mops, they carried out the endless campaign against dirt.

We also had another occupant of the house, certainly not a servant but not family either. This was Matron, a woman employed to look after the boys' health. Matron held a surgery every day, to which boys could come if they were ill.

The big drawback of Matron, as my mother often mentioned out of her hearing, was that as soon as there was a flu epidemic, Matron was invariably its first victim. My mother then had to take over her role, without the nurse-training that made it possible to do the job with confidence.

In the big flu epidemic of 1957-58, so many people were ill that my mother accepted my offer to take meals on trays to the victims on their sickbeds. In the normal way, for us to enter a boy's room while he was in bed would have been unacceptable to her, but this was an emergency.

CHAPTER 5 – THE BOYS

The boys who in term time lived in Bradbys were a very mixed lot. In the late 1940s, twin sons of the Maharajah of Jaipur enrolled in the school. Good looks and charm were the characteristics I knew about, but no doubt there were other sides to them. Some boys were sent to Harrow from the USA, others from the London business community. We had farmers' sons, sons of my father's colleagues and scions of a Greek shipping company. There were people whose parents made frequent appearances in gossip columns, and boys whose parents were shy, retiring and self-effacing. The notorious Lady Docker appeared in a gold-plated Rolls on Speech Day. Titled boys from stately homes rubbed shoulders with boys on full scholarships from local suburbs. One of "our boys" was from a famous Bristol wine merchant family.

A long list of rules dominated the boys' lives. A lot of them related to smoking and drinking, others were about unauthorised absence from the Hill and sartorial privileges accorded to different groups in the school also featured. Chapel was compulsory, unless you were a Roman Catholic.

Manners were regarded as immensely important. My parents struggled to develop these in boys, initially regarded as "louts". The aim was to produce boys who could cope in all circumstances, who would be gentlemanly, industrious, mature and successful.

The reality, of course, was quite different. The boys had between them, most of the full range of human frailty, and their behaviour often fell short of the ideal. Discipline was maintained sometimes with difficulty. Corporal punishment sometimes took place.

In an obituary of my father published in "The Harrovian," it was said that my father's only fault was sometimes thinking too well of boys. In a book of his, I found a pencilled note from Hamlet: "To thine own self be true."

Throughout my childhood, homosexual relationships remained illegal and, in any case, the boys in my father's house were mostly minors, with whom gay affairs would have been seen as illegal even today. At times, issues over the boys' sexuality surfaced and had to be confronted by those charged with their care.

Not that any of this was discussed in front of us, the children. We simply became aware of it, in the same way that we knew when there was an affair between a master and another master's wife.

The boys' emotions often aroused our sympathy. At the beginning of autumn terms, one would see very small new boys, in their very new uniforms, wandering about alone on Sunday afternoons, looking the embodiment of loneliness. One hoped each of them quickly found friends, but one was powerless to act.

CHAPTER 6 – THEATRICALS, MUSIC AND SCOTTISH DANCING

Every summer at Harrow a Shakespeare play was performed. Boys took all the parts including those of female characters. The plays were produced by Ronald Watkins. There was very little scenery. With the stage jutting out into the audience, who sat in a semi-circle round it, acting was almost "in the round". Curtains, a balcony, the odd prop and few spotlights, plus Tudor clothes were the accessories for the actors and the verse they were speaking.

Not to be outdone, the Old Harrovians also produced a Shakespeare play most years. Once or twice, there was a Gilbert and Sullivan operetta done by the masters. For several years, I watched these rather passively as a member of the audience. But one summer, the Old Harrovians needed peasant girls who would dance for their production of "A Winter's Tale".

I was invited to take part and attended some rehearsals for the dancing. At the first of these, I was given an only slightly garbled version of the plot by a master's son I knew.

The wardrobe-person decreed that I must wear a long bulky skirt made of sacking, which was intended to resemble homespun. There was some kind of jacket or bodice and a small wreath of flowers on my brushed-back hair. These heavy garments gave me insight into how people must have sweltered in an Elizabethan summer.

Feeling a strong bout of stage fright, my companions and I danced the English Renaissance measure on the rough coconut matting of the stage to unfamiliar music on early instruments.

These productions of Shakespeare were intended to resemble as closely as possible those done at Shakespeare's Globe on the South Bank in the late sixteenth century. Without the lavish physical resources of the modern commercial theatre, Shakespeare's verse became, as it should be, the whole point.

In the year when the play selected was "Hamlet", a seventeen-year-old boy in my father's house played the hero. He was Alexander Schouvalov. To learn his enormous part, he was given some time off lessons. It was something those who saw it never forgot; he was so much nearer in age to the true age of the hero than, say, Olivier in the film released in 1948. Sir Laurence Olivier, as he later became, was forty-one when the film was made.

Other performances took place in the bosky gardens of the boys' houses. In a darkening space between the looming dark-red brick of the building and the groups of shrubs and trees heavy with July foliage, Shaw entered my consciousness. It was "Androcles and the Lion". To the west, on the audience's left, the sun went down behind trees and rooftops. The lion must have been immensely hot in his plush fur animal outfit. The hero, a tailor in Ancient Rome about to be thrown to the lions for the amusement of an audience eager to see bloodshed, was played by a master's son, David Warr.

The Captain of the centurions asks, "What is God?" Lavinia, a Christian about to be killed by wild animals, answers "When we know that, Captain, we shall be Gods ourselves." An exchange which wound itself into my brain and surfaced whenever God was under discussion.

When I first heard about the music competitions, held each July, I went along to listen. These were held on Sunday afternoons. Through the arched window of the music schools, one could see summer sky and dream listening to the pieces. Only a small group of boys competed for each prize. The generous endowments and donations of prizes made to the school meant several prizes rather than one.

The adjudicator was Dame Ruth Railton, of the National Youth Orchestra. In this setting, I first heard "O star of Eve" from Tannhauser, sung by a boy with a glorious voice. That experience gave me a lifelong devotion to Wagner.

Each Easter Term, the school sang in an oratorio. Soloists were invited to sing the lead parts in Elijah, The Messiah, the German Requiem of Brahms or The Creation. The whole school of five hundred boys sang the choruses. The volume of sound produced by the school orchestra, hundreds of male voices and the organ defied description.

Female voices for the choir were provided by local residents, house matrons, masters' wives and daughters. Seated behind the orchestra, we could observe, at very close quarters, the dedicated behaviour of the instrumentalists.

Taking part, as a humble chorus member, in those mighty works, magnified my sense of being part of a community, here a creative one. Such happenings drew together people with a very wide variation in their understanding of music. Taking part in the playing of an oratorio was something done for our own pleasure and that of others. It represented co-operative effort by about seven hundred and fifty people.

Without ever being a pupil officially enrolled on the list of people educated at Harrow, I was thus able to benefit from being present at all the cultural events laid on for the boys in which I felt any interest. Amateur productions certainly, but accurate pointers to the wealth of European music, art and literature I spent a lot of my life getting to know.

Those studies led to new encounters with Russian, Canadian, American, and African novels, poetry, music and pictures.

Life was not as solemn as may appear from what I have said above.

Scottish Dancing was a big feature of our early lives. There were, and are, numerous groups all over Britain who enjoy this vigorous form of exercise. Some members are expatriate Scots nostalgic for their native heaths; others are simply lovers of Scottish culture.

One of the leading exponents of the art at Harrow was the late Tim Warr. His memorable Rat Hunts, intended as a rival attraction for those who could not afford Hunt Balls in the Christmas holiday, were a great attraction on New Year's Eve. Held in the school gym, with candles in bottles providing the lighting, they featured many different Scottish dances.

There were many informal occasions each school holiday, held in house libraries and the Red House in Middle Road, which belonged to John Lyon School, when Scottish dancing was indulged in, often with more enthusiasm than skill.

My late brother-in-law, Michael Argyle, a psychologist, who researched the ways in which people could become happy, recommended the activity very highly. Combining as it did vigorous movement, catchy music, social interaction, laughter when things went wrong, and the acquiring of a skill, it seemed to him the ideal leisure activity.

For us, our Scottish roots on our mother's side may have been an additional incentive. But so was the chance to get at rather closer quarters to boys than we normally did.

What struck one most forcibly about Scottish dancing was that if you made a mistake and moved in the wrong direction, there was never time to put it right. The music moved on so fast that one could not. Everybody's mistakes generated laughter. The speed of it made it unlike most other things I did; at least when writing or painting something there was time for second thoughts.

Clothes for this activity were varied. This era of the late 1950s was well before jeans became the uniform for everything and everyone.

I believe we wore skirts, sometimes, even the Mackintosh kilt which had come down to us from some ancestor. One evening, when we were due at a neighbour's for Scottish dancing, I remember being in a state of extreme impatience to set off, because we were delayed by Joanna not being able to decide what to wear.

CHAPTER 7 – BOOKS

My initial belief that I would never master the art of reading luckily proved overly pessimistic.

The public library in Harrow gave me a sizeable chunk of my education.

It lay at the foot of the hill, just across the railway lines. It was an unprepossessing, single-storey building, rather resembling a prefab. On its right, the tube line ran to central London in one direction, and out to Metroland and the Chiltern Hills in the other. The rumble of trains shook the building constantly and disturbed one's browsing. The stark lighting, wall-like bookcases and absence of interior decoration were disincentives to read. The idea that libraries should be user-friendly had certainly not caught on. The library building expressed the austerity of the age in which it was built, but also the hunger for knowledge.

In those days, libraries were only about books. Videos, records, reading groups, visits by authors, computer-use and newspapers were all in the future.

There were several aisles of very tall bookcases, with lino floors between them. No carpets, easy chairs or screens on which to consult to see whether the library had a particular book.

Children were tolerated, but no more. They had some slightly lower shelves.

By the time I was twelve, I had read everything in the children's section which attracted me, sometimes reading the same book several times. Noel Streatfield's novels about a family of three girls were a favourite. There was a lot about ballet in them and about aspiring to be famous. The effort to appear in the right clothes despite lack of money was a big theme in the books.

I then ventured into the adult section and borrowed many books, some of them well over my head. My only partial grasp of their contents did not deter me, and I went back very often, sometimes two or three times a week.

Clutching my books, I would set out on the return walk. The route lay past a very old-fashioned sweetshop. Even in the early 1950s, it seemed dated. It sold treacle toffee. This ambrosial substance became part of a library trip.

I always hoped, on those walks, to avoid the moments when a bell would chime and suddenly the streets would be thronged with five hundred boys going from one lesson to another. I was embarrassed to be engulfed in this flood tide of chattering males.

Our parents had very definite views on what we ought to read. The usual diet of Beatrix Potter, Orlando the Marmalade Cat and Hans Anderson became familiar to us. But why did we never have Dr Doolittle, Winnie the Pooh or the Jungle Book? Friends often mentioned these titles to us, and yet we never read them. Joanna loved the Arthur Ransome books. I found them unbearably tedious and greatly dependent on knowledge of, and interest in, the mysteries of sailing.

The question of why a book appealed to some and not others hardly disturbed me at all until I was much older.

I was given books about figures such as Helen Keller, Florence Nightingale and Elizabeth Fry. The message seemed to be that women could achieve things, but you had to have what it takes, and probably not be a wife and mother.

These books, about heroines who became household names, gave me a realisation that you had to have a robust belief in yourself.

Another book I was given was "Seven Queens of England". That did interest me and, in due course, political history did dominate the history syllabus at school.

Later, I found social history much more to my taste. Who could argue that the aeroplane, the pill and the washing machine had had as big an effect as Magna Carta and the Domesday Book?

Some small books full of brilliant colour first came out in the 1930s. Margaret Tarrant's Flower Fairies of the Autumn and several other titles really appealed to me. Although to an adult they no doubt appeared whimsical and inappropriate as an introduction to botany, the beautiful, accurate paintings of the plants meant that in later years I had no trouble identifying spindleberry and bryony when they showed up in country hedges.

Comics were very big in our lives up to the age of twelve or so. I had one called "School Friend", which had numerous strip cartoons, mostly black and white, a few with a third colour. Joanna had one called "Girl" the female counterpart of the more famous and older "Eagle".

In this, there were many improving stores about heroes and heroines. It was more intelligently written than School Friend, and some of the stories were by Chad Varah, later (1953) founder of the Samaritans.

We were devoted to these publications. But we also pored over two magazines our parents took. The first was "The Illustrated London News". This showed the news largely in sepia photographs with very short captions. Being a person for whom the image was as important as the word, I found the wealth of drawings and photographs of absorbing delight.

Each year's issues finished with the Christmas number. Instead of the monochrome images so redolent of the 50s, at least some pages were in full colour. Old master paintings were reproduced in their rich, seductive tones. There were modern paintings too. This was where I first saw work by Rowland Hilder and Eliot Hodgkin, two fine artists I've now admired for over half a century. It is hard to over-estimate the sensuous pleasure of seeing these coloured reproductions after so much non-colour.

Then there was Vogue, which my mother took from the 30s to her death in 1984. It was full of photographs of extremely slim models in unattainably expensive outfits: ball dresses, suits, casual clothes and cocktail frocks. Yearning to look like that, we hadn't yet realised that we never would. We entered a fantasy world as we looked at it, a world in which women didn't have a hair out of place.

Vogue also contained high-quality journalism on cultural subjects and even cooking, a topic I was beginning to find worth exploring. The glossy pages, sometimes in colour, introduced me to the idea of elegance, something I always admired in others but never achieved for myself.

My mother didn't often read new books, but she did read reviews of them in the Times. One title which excited her attention was Rachel Carson's "The Silent Spring", a polemic against agro-chemicals and a description of the effects of these on bird populations.

The reviews she read convinced her that the world was going down hill fast. Birds and flowers, which had been common in her childhood, were now rare. It was a highly important book, but she never felt a need to read it, only to know that there was such a book.

My father did his best to interest us in contemporary culture. He took us to see "Waiting for Godot", which we found mystifying.

But the recommendation he made which had the most dramatic and long-term effect on my life was when, in the mid 1950s, he told me to read "On the Beach".

This was a novel by Neville Shute about how human life might come to an end after a nuclear war.

With the possible exception of "Jude the Obscure", which I read in 1962 and have never had the courage to read again, no book in my entire life affected me as deeply as this one. After my reading of it, when I was about fifteen, I became convinced that nuclear war was inevitable and that the destruction of mankind would follow.

In this reading, it looked as if we would have no adulthood, or if we did, that it would be our dreadful duty to kill our children to save them from slow starvation and radiation sickness. It followed that all the effort of working at school would be pointless, that there would be neither permanency nor continuity.

As teenagers do, I over-reacted. Nowadays, it might be said I was depressed because I couldn't see a future. Why didn't I talk to my parents about how likely the events predicted were to happen? I don't know.

I lacked someone to say to me, "Not every disaster someone foresees actually comes to pass." For me, it seemed all too likely.

So, I was very sympathetic to anti-nuclear demonstrations, like the Aldermaston marches. On one of them, I did walk some of the way but lacked the staying power and confidence to do the whole thing.

A very large number of my contemporaries thought the same way; that they wanted to live their lives and not be snuffed out before they'd had a chance to do so. It was an idea which united us.

The end result was that I found "On the Beach" far more vivid, frightening, convincing and powerful than any Dickens or Shakespeare I was expected to study at school.

When I was ten and Joanna thirteen, Everest was climbed. My father bought the book recounting the historic achievement. Joanna, being very geographical, read the whole thing. The part I found most interesting was the fascinating list of tinned foods which the mountaineers took with them.

Some of the books which mattered to me were ones which my mother had read in her childhood.

"Little Women", first published in 1868, was one of them. The interactions between the four sisters were definitely something I and my sisters could relate to. Perhaps we considered the plot outlandish; children and young people didn't die, did they? Or if they did, surely only in the nineteenth century? I found the death of Beth deeply affecting, as it was meant to be.

"Black Beauty" was another book I could never re-read. The cruelty in it, I later learned, was intended to bring about changes in the way horses were treated in the nineteenth century. In 1877, when it first appeared, the economy was greatly dependent upon the horse.

"The Secret Garden" was a favourite. As a child, one enjoys great books by taking them at face value. Later, one becomes aware of their underlying philosophy.

In it, Mary, the spoilt indoor-living child, orphaned by cholera in India, receives from Dickon, the Yorkshire child brought up to appreciate nature, the gift of emotional health. This comes from learning how to grow things, and from contact with Dickon's unselfconsciously "normal" family. Since my later years have been partly devoted to growing things, first from necessity and later for pleasure, it was maybe the distant memories of this book which stayed in my mind.

"What Katy Did" and the sequel, "What Katy Did Next" I read many times. She was a tomboy, which I also was, tearing my skirts climbing over fences and getting into trouble for it. Her impressions of life were so vividly described, and her trials, travels and family life were beautifully put together.

The first book I ever enthused about though, was "The Wind in the Willows". At six, I went home from school and told my mother we'd had such a lovely book read to us. My parents bought me a copy in which I coloured all the line illustrations. We read it, the same copy, to our sons twenty years later, and forty years later, to our grandson.

It was an age of censorship. In 1954, when I was eleven, 167,000 books were burned for obscenity. In 1960, on the other hand, when the tide had turned, decisively, after the Lady Chatterley trial, one could read just about anything without being prevented. We had gone from having censorship imposed on us, to being allowed to decide for ourselves. It was a sign that the 60s were going to be different from the 50s.

My parents were quite sure we should know some poetry. When I was six, my father offered me some trifling reward if I would learn by heart Tennyson's "The Brook".

I duly did so and discovered that you could find pictures among the words. As I added gradually to the verses stored in my head, I gained intoxicating feelings of power; these words had been written in other ages, had been made memorable and would live on in people's memories.

The first poem I learned contained a simple idea — that people come and go but landscape and nature go on forever — which in the 1940s seemed uncontroversial. Now I know nature will only continue if we allow it to.

That poem stayed with me all my life. After retiring, I was finally able to visit Somersby in Lincolnshire (this was in the course of a pilgrimage to several places) where Tennyson had been born in the rectory in 1809. In the church were tapestries of places which had been important to him, among them the local brook.

We descended a hill and found, under a bower of leaves, the simple bridge with water chuckling beneath it. My enjoyment of the poem was finally complete.

Or was it? Perhaps it was only when I'd read "The Brook" to my grandson, Laurence, and got him to memorise the couplet which ends each section, that my debt to my father was finally repaid.

The poem was thus a bridge between my father, born 1908, and my grandson, born 1995.

My father's battered copy, with his name and 1938 written inside it, of the Dragon Book of Verse, became the book I turned to in my childhood and adolescence to discover English verse. And I still turn to it today. Its condition confirms that it has been more used than any other volume in the house. Dog-eared, spineless, surviving several moves; it was his legacy to me.

CHAPTER 8 — CLOTHES

In my childhood and my teenage years, if you needed some item of clothing you went out with your mother, who chose it with you, paid for it and then went home with you and you both got on with something else.

Shopping for clothes was not then an all-consuming reason for living, as it has since become for some people. No doubt in those days, some people bought things they couldn't afford, but the vast scale of debt throughout society today was unheard of.

In the 1940s, we had sagging wool "bathing costumes" as they were known. These took ages to dry after use, and either shrank or stretched. They always came in sober colours like black or navy blue.

With the 1950s came the advent of what we learned to call "swimsuits", streamlined nylon numbers, in just about any colour, which dried in a flash and never shrank.

The bikini also burst on the scene, but with our puppy fat, we would have looked terrible in them. At second hand, we heard that they were fine for lazing on a beach but distinctly insecure for serious swimming.

Out of school, for seaside holidays, we had shapeless shorts, Aertex blouses and hand-knitted or Marks and Spencer pullovers (Pullovers were called "jerseys" in those days. The word "sweater" didn't reach us from America until the mid 1950s), worn with sandals or "sensible" walking shoes. Gym shoes were nothing like the modern trainer, but useful if we were invited to sail in someone's dinghy. We wore Wellingtons for any messy activity, into which we changed from our "walking shoes". There were laced and usually chestnut-coloured leather.

My first school, in that respect progressive, had no uniform. School photographs show smocked dresses, plain blouses and skirts and simple outfits usually in rather quiet "good-taste" colours.

My only other school, North London Collegiate, had a rigidly enforced uniform policy. Woe betide us if we were seen without our brown felt school berets. The rest of our outfits were as sexless as possible: gabardine raincoats, pale beige school blouses and dark brown tunics. In summer, we wore brown check gingham dresses, which may have been practical but did not flatter us.

The only item of my school uniform that I really liked was our royal-blue linen overalls, which had to be worn for art, science and pottery. These were cut in a smock design dating back several decades. I found these all-enveloping garments rather endearing, firstly because they were in my favourite colour. Secondly, putting them on opening up new worlds of art lessons in a proper studio and science lessons in a proper laboratory.

I made very little use of the latter opportunity. O-level biology was the only science in which I reached any recognisable standard, probably because I found drawing the diagrams easier than some people did.

We also wore these overalls for cookery. Looking back on how much of my marriage I spent in a kitchen, perhaps those lessons were of the greatest use of anything I was taught. A lady called Constance Kitchen taught us — her career must have been meant.

She also taught us simple sewing. From these beginnings came the ambitions of several of my friends to make their own clothes. It was a time of "can do" philosophy; it was worth having a go at something if it looked achievable.

I mentioned the buying of clothes. But in our childhood, nothing was ever bought if there was a garment which could be "passed on" from a cousin, or older and bigger friend, or an older sister. Clothes were a valuable resource during the war and post-war years, and children's clothes were hardly ever used by only one wearer.

My earliest garments were hand-knitted baby clothes made by my mother, and small dresses she had carefully stitched together. Finding a box of these when emptying my sister's flat following her death gave me a pang of realisation of how much effort she had gone to.

71

Throwing them away gave me even more of a pang. If there had not been such haste to clear the flat, I might have got round to realising they belonged in a museum. They represented an age where in the absence of goods in the shops, people fell back on those skills their ancestors had acquired over the centuries, which had only been lost when factory-made mass-market goods became available in the shops.

Our consciousness of the world of fashion was raised by the catalogues, which came through the letterbox addressed to our mother. Each of the big London department stores sent one.

They were illustrated by drawings showing the clothes for sale flattered by impossibly slim and elongated figures. This led to immediate disappointment; on one's own dumpy build, the dress, ideal on paper, looked as inelegant as all the old clothes in anyone's wardrobe.

We used to pore over these catalogues for hours. Every dress, coat, blouse or skirt came in several colours. What is reseda green? What is petrol blue? we would ask. Evening and wedding dresses especially grabbed our attention. They belonged to a dream-world of maturity and sophistication we ugly-ducklings could not enter.

Every month, a copy of "Vogue" came through the letterbox. My mother hid it until she'd read it herself and then we were allowed to look at it. In the glossy pages were photographs of apparitions of beauty and elegance. The articles, dense areas of small print, purported to give the woman about town a smattering of cultural knowledge. A fictitious, very slim white-haired woman called "Mrs Exeter", was photographed in expensive clothes for the older woman, which my mother, though only forty in 1950, rather hankered after.

Of course, the world of Vogue was an unreal one. At any rate, the world of having one's hair done often, of having diamonds and rubies presented to one, of shopping routinely at Harrods, Harvey Nichols and Liberty's, never became my world. It encouraged a materialist and consumerist outlook at odds with the rest of our upbringing.

The subtext was that if you didn't dress in a certain way, discarding the previous season's clothes and acquiring new ones, you wouldn't pass muster or be capable of attracting men. My sisters became so hooked on glossy magazines as a result of these early experiences that, when my mother died, they continued to take copious supplies of glossy magazines themselves.

There were other distinct differences in the way we were dressed and equipped from children of today. We used proper handkerchiefs to blow our noses, not tissues. The washing of these handkerchiefs was a great business, involving boiling them in a superannuated saucepan, washing them, hanging them out on the washing line, ironing them accurately into squares, and stacking them in neat piles.

The advent of nylon, and its wide availability as the 50s advanced, was hailed as a great leap forward by my mother. That you did not have to iron it was a miracle. In 1954, the year I was eleven, she asked the lady who sometimes ran up clothes for her to make me a dress of crushed strawberry nylon with a full skirt. I was overjoyed. It was worn for the first time at Harrow Speech Day in June, and I ran down the outside wooden staircase which led from our drawing room to the garden, with the air rushing up my skirts and making them whirl around me.

Other man-made fibres also thrilled her: Dacron, acrilan and terylene all represented to her generation liberation from the arduous business of keeping clothes clean and ironed. Only later came the natural-fabrics backlash. Years afterwards, people rediscovered silk, linen, cotton and wool and declared them infinitely superior.

Other things in our physical lives were still quite primitive. Washing our hair happened in the bathroom basin. To dry it, we knelt by an electric fire with a big fireguard in front of it. Nonetheless, we still sometimes got too close and there was a smell of singed hair. Hairdryers were non-existent, except as big machines we knew people sat under in hairdressing shops.

As children, our hair was cut in a straight shape all round our heads, fastened with a ribbon or slide, which often fell off or got lost. If your hair was long, you had plaits; these were done in the morning by your mother and entailed the hair being pulled tightly to divide into three bunches on each side. I hated it, squirmed and asked to have my hair short.

When we became teenagers, my mother was very firm about what was proper. You could not have an obviously protruding bottom; a girdle must be worn to flatten it. "You're not going out dressed like that?" was a remark with several variations I heard quite often in my mid to late teens.

Her dogmatic outlook was made partly explicable by the knowledge that, when she first lived in Harrow in the summer of 1939, you could not be seen walking down the High Street without a hat on.

Although the war did away with many beliefs about correct clothing, some lingered on. My mother was certain that one must never be provocatively dressed. The girdles she insisted on were desperately uncomfortable. When you wore one under trousers it rode up and formed a tight restrictive band around the waist. When I became old enough to choose, I never wore one again. She, however, remained faithful to them.

CHAPTER 9 – FOOD

In those distant times, food was always something in season. Strawberries could only be had in June and July; they were grown in the open rather than in today's polytunnels. They were not flown in from tropical places to provide winter desserts.

The rhythm of the seasons created variety. Freezers barely existed in the domestic environment, and they certainly weren't at all common. In the 50s, some people didn't even have fridges.

We did have a fridge, though we didn't eat from them, very often. Producing a meal meant doing things to raw ingredients until they were edible. There were no "ready-meals". Convenience foods, like fish and chips, existed and were popular. There were no take-aways from curry houses or Chinese restaurants, no pizzerias with motorcycle deliverymen. If you wanted to eat, generally speaking, you had to cook.

Food in 40s and 50s Britain, before the revolutionary advent of Elizabeth David, has suffered a bad press. But not all cooking was bad and you often ate very well in a home where the person cooking was really interested in food. There was also far less waste of perfectly good food than there is today. People were very conscious after the shortages of the war years that all items bought with the weekly housekeeping money needed to be used economically and effectively.

There was also a much greater level of making things at home rather than buying them than there is today. People picked blackberries and made pies, they produced their own marmalade, they baked a cake not only when visitors were due but regularly for hungry children. They boiled chicken carcasses for soup, they used up leftover cabbage and potato to make bubble and squeak, a dish which can be utterly delicious. Our housekeeping cost less because we made so many things at home.

Intensive farming had hardly begun. Pigs roamed in fields, cows and their calves meditated in meadows and chickens were all free-range. The sins of battery production and intensive rearing brought about a lowering not only in price but also in quality.

The breakfasts I remember from the 1950s were cooked ones. On Sundays at Bradbys, we always had pork sausages. Each one was served on a rectangle of fried bread, brown with dripping. No sausages I have eaten in the half-century since came anywhere near those ones; dark brown and crispy on the outside, meltingly flavourful within and comfortingly hot, a glorious start to the seventh day.

Of course, they were full of fat and salt. But we walked so much more than modern children do that maybe the effect of these was mitigated.

Then there was rice pudding, which we had quite often. I loved it. It was made with whole milk and had a rich brown crust. Inside it was golden, perhaps with the addition of eggs. Each rice grain was swollen with the full-fat milk in which it had been cooked.

Sausages and rice pudding, two deeply unfashionable items today, but memorable foods, evoking a childhood in which we appreciated their filling bulk and their warming qualities.

Another dish which I remember nostalgically was rissoles. These were little croquettes, made of meat, perhaps left over from the Sunday joint, minced and mixed with diced vegetables. They were then shaped into fat sausage-like pieces, dipped in egg and breadcrumbs, and then fried.

If they had been made in France, they would have been called "croquettes" and acquired dignity, and been appreciated as a savoury way of being careful not to waste leftovers. Being British, they were possibly despised. But I liked them.

With them, we were expected to eat "greens". Cabbage, in all its variety, was one such; a vegetable many people hardly touch today.

It wasn't haute cuisine. But it was nutritious and satisfying. We all grew taller than our mother had been. There were no fizzy drinks, we rarely saw a crisp, and the burger had not reached our shores from the USA. Obesity was quite rare compared with today.

On the long journey home from my secondary school (a walk, followed by a bus journey, followed by another walk), I dreamed hungrily of Fry's chocolate cream. This was a bar of my favourite plain chocolate, with inside a filling of white vanilla cream. My quickly growing body craved it and more often than not my pocket money was spent on it.

A favourite which very occasionally appeared in our house was Fuller's walnut cake. This was a small, deep round cake, a sponge with three layers each separated from the other by a layer of white icing, and a complete covering of the same. Walnut fragments were scattered through it and five or six half walnuts decorated the top.

A couple of times I stayed with Joanna at my great aunt's house in Sussex. Great Aunts Elsie and Katie were very elderly, not well off, kind most of the time but with rigid views.

When I asked, aged eight or nine, quite innocently, what was for lunch, I was told, "You mustn't think only of your stomach."

Their personal history, Katie as a missionary in Africa, Elsie as a dutiful daughter who had spent her life selflessly caring for ailing and ageing relations, I only learned about as an adult.

Perhaps it was my first intimation that other people had different priorities and values. Later on, I learned from my mother that the two old great aunts had lived, for some time, on £11 a month. There was uncertainty as to when in the twentieth century this had been the case, but it would not have been much at any time.

Every evening, my aunts knelt on the sitting room floor, surrounded by an Edward Bawden wallpaper design of camels traversing sand dunes. Aunt Elsie said the prayer which starts "Lighten our darkness…". The beams of the setting sun entered the room from far away across Sussex.

After prayers, we were sent to bed. Our aunts must, after all, have realised that food actually was quite important to children, because by the big double bed Joanna and I shared, was a tin of biscuits, coloured and with animal shapes printed on them, in case we were hungry in the night.

In today's affluent Britain, it is hard to believe that over seventy years ago, those of us lucky enough to have friends or relations in Australia or New Zealand received food parcels to eke out our rations. The dried fruit we couldn't get here was greatly welcome, without it there couldn't have been anything resembling Christmas cake or pudding. The food parcel also featured in the lives of prisoners of war in German camps, and perhaps enabled them to have something to which they could look forward.

It has been said that some British people were on the verge of starvation during the war. This may in part have been because mothers diverted to their children their own ration of foodstuffs. If so, it was a sacrifice of which we should be conscious.

When my parents had visitors there was wine with the meal, but not otherwise. Today's huge consumption of wine, spirits and beer was unheard of. The "working man's pint" was the foundation of the fortunes of brewers, but large-scale binge drinking, so much a feature of city life today, just did not happen. Of course, there were alcoholics, but not people in their twenties or thirties with advanced liver disease. Thrift and restraint were much more marked in the time of which I write.

CHAPTER 10 – HOLIDAYS

It was looked upon in the early 1950s as rather exotic to have your holiday abroad. Even if you could arrange it, no one was allowed to take more than £25 a head out of the country, which rather restricted the options.

Unless you had friends or relations abroad with whom you could stay, it was very difficult to go. So, families went to stay by the sea or in the country, in hotels or rented cottages or houses. Camping and caravanning were also popular.

We accepted the frightfulness of some British summer weather as being the price which had to be paid. Some bucket and spade holidays in Dorset when I was under ten were followed by two or three years of caravanning on the Suffolk coast at Walsberswick.

Camping in the 1950s was extremely primitive compared with today. There were no extravagantly equipped camper vans. We had canvas tents which leaked when it rained, sleeping bags and a ground sheet.

Our loo was a hole in the ground, a wooden seat and a square canvas tent. Washing facilities in the remote fields selected by my parents at Shipton Gorge were a kettle of boiling water and an enamel basin.

Food was cooked by my father over a Primus stove. My father adored officiating as cook. We were given bread to soak up the juices left by the meat. He also did sausages and there was the annual treat of a visit from a travelling fish and chip shop.

When the primus stove was finally turned off, following my parents' enamel mugs of tea, and the loud noise it made suddenly stopped, we could hear again the silence of the countryside.

If it rained, as in Dorset it often did, I was disconsolate. On one occasion, it poured so relentlessly that our heavy ancient Rolls became stuck in the mud when we went to an agricultural show. I was aghast; what would happen if we could not get the car out? How would we get home?

Resourceful farmers all around us sized up the situation and hauled the car out of the mud by attaching it to a tractor.

The beach, pebbly as it was, was our Mecca. Each morning and afternoon, my father bought us all an ice cream, something that would never have happened on an ordinary day at home. We became aquatic creatures, devoted to the shoreline with its thrilling and unfamiliar dangers, like jellyfish.

In 1953, Dorset was still a county where the cut corn was arranged in flopping stooks to dry in the sun. These stood in a regular pattern of parallel lines receding into the distance, just as the cut hay was left two or three months earlier. These patterns gave texture to the sandy-coloured stubble fields.

My parents had stayed in the county when courting in the 1930s and felt it had not changed much since then. The combined village shop and post office in Burton Bradstock was a dark, small room smelling of bacon and cheese and selling all manner of goods.

In the later 1950s, my parents rented some houses in Scotland. In 1958, it was a minister's house at the Loch Ness end of Glen Affric.

One day of this holiday, while out on a walk, we met a South African dentist on holiday in the area.

He asked if he might drive us three girls up Glen Affric to watch the sunset.

My parents agreed, but my mother said, just before he drove us away, "Be careful — they are all we've got."

He was careful. All the way up the glen, he told us about his life in South Africa, and about his girlfriend. She was, he said, what all women ought to be like. "Soft and gentle, with just a bit of fire."

I was overly impressed. No one I had met up to that time had ever made pronouncements about what all women ought to be like. I had not even realised that this could be a topic.

The more I thought about his comment, the more I wondered if I, or my sisters, could ever be said to have attained this ideal of womanhood.

I never at the time realised that perhaps there could be other definitions of the perfect woman, articulated by very different kinds of people from the South African dentist.

Nor did I ever begin to construct a model of the ideal man.

But why has that remark stayed in my mind for more than fifty years, when hundreds of other things said to me have been forgotten?

Perhaps it was something to do with the setting; mounting higher and higher on a very narrow road with flaming sky stretched above the rocky peaks was memorably impressive. At the top, the sunset, as he predicted it would be, was magnificent. He drove us safely down. We never saw him again.

Driving to Scotland from Middlesex was a very different experience from today. Pre-motorway, the journeys were immensely long. The A1 went through every town on the way, instead of round towns, as now. That meant long waits at traffic lights and slow driving through thirty mph zones.

Highland roads were in a much more primitive state than now, with poor surfaces and potholes. It was also so different from the tidy, tame southeast.

My parents thought we should know the land of our birth. They dutifully escorted us to Stonehenge, Hatfield House, Maiden Castle and any other historic site, which happened to be en route for our holiday.

They took us one April on a trip to the Welsh Marches. Here, I visited Stokesay, Presteigne and Ludlow for the first time. Sheep grazing in sunset fields at Stokesay struck one especially. They seemed to represent the peace and continuity of rural life.

On an earlier holiday, caravanning in Suffolk, I'd written a story in an exercise book. I didn't repeat the experiment. By fifteen, I'd learned what I didn't know at twelve, that I hadn't read enough or written enough to be able to produce a novel.

When I reached seventeen, in 1960, my parents did manage to take us to France. Perhaps they'd had a legacy. Going abroad was now a pleasure many people were able to experience, some for the first time.

With that first venture across the Channel, a chapter in our lives ended. It was the last time all five of us went somewhere together. British holidays, in the company of parents and sisters, became something on which to look back nostalgically.

But the holidays in Britain, which were such a feature of 50s life, had an immensely beneficial result; we knew something about our own country. The extraordinary variety of landscapes and townscapes in Britain was something to enjoy and remember. It was the cultural background of the many strands of the family which had come together to produce, firstly, my parents and, then, us.

Knowing some of the different regions of Britain meant that, when we finally were able to look at parts of Europe, we were able to appreciate their differentness.

"What should they know of England, who only England know?" asked Kipling. My mother quoted this to us many times.

CHAPTER 11 – CHRISTMAS

Having battled with their unpredictable staff and with whatever disciplinary problems the boys had caused during the term, my parents must have been tired out by the end of the long Christmas term.

But we children were completely unaware of that. We thought of the presents we would like for Christmas and made wholly unrealistic lists. For years, mine started with "a pony". I had no idea how much these cost to buy or maintain, let alone how large a paddock would be needed to keep one in.

Because, unlike modern children, we were never given presents except at birthdays and Christmas, we looked forward to these festivals with enormous hope.

With a child's imperfect grasp of vocabulary and from attendance at numerous carol services at all the family's different schools, I picked up the words and tunes of the better-known carols. "Hark the Harrow Angels Sing" was one of my favourites.

When I was teenaged, I, my sisters and several friends, led by the vicar and two of his five children, went carol-singing after dark several evenings before Christmas.

In the frosty starlight, carrying a lantern or two to read the words by, we trooped from West Street to Crown Street, alongside terraces and up alleys. We sang a carol at each stop. So, Christmas came in, with the central notion of what Christmas was not yet forgotten.

My mother's insistence that we should listen, every Christmas Eve, to the broadcast carols from King's College, Cambridge, meant that we knew from an early age what spiritual and artistic heights choral singing could reach. The words of the nine lessons, each read by a person representing a particular aspect of Cambridge life, became part of our common heritage.

Like most other children, we found it hard to get to sleep on Christmas Eve. On waking, we found one of my mother's thick stockings on each of our beds, with several bulges in them. There was always gold-wrapped chocolate money, a tangerine and sometimes a cherished piece of my mother's doll's house furniture.

After breakfast, we went to church at St Mary's. On our return, my Uncle Kenneth and his four children, Alastair, Lindsay, Andrew and Moray, arrived for lunch. My Aunt Elizabeth was never there. "Not well" was the explanation. It was only much later that I learned that she was an alcoholic and that the provision of Christmas dinner for her family was quite beyond her.

We adored Alastair, who was several years older than we were, and a pilot in the Fleet Air Arm. Lindsay was a medical student and combed the hair of two little

89

boys, correcting their manners. Andrew and Moray wore Mackintosh dark green and scarlet kilts, but we only had eyes for Alastair, who combined glamour and charm more brilliantly than almost any human being I have ever known.

Alastair was full of fun and laughter. He was also very clever and passed out of Dartmouth Naval College with the highest marks in his year. We wished he could have been our elder brother.

The two cooks being on a well-earned holiday, my mother cooked the turkey herself, carved by my father at the big mahogany table. We must have looked like a large Victorian family; five Mackintoshes and five Thompsons.

In the centre of the table were small filigree silver dishes containing chocolates for the end of the meal and the crackers we would shortly pull. I learned to enjoy the traditional delights of Christmas pudding, made to an ancient family recipe.

We became impatient with the grown-ups' desire to sit and talk and left the table. For a number of Christmases, there was a vogue for mixed hockey on the Harrow School parade ground. With twenty or so a side and walking sticks as well as hockey sticks, it was a fast game dominated by male friends who shone at other sports too.

As a completely non-sporty girl, I watched in amazement as the boys took over the game displaying their expertise. The unorthodox tarmac surface, and even more unorthodox slope, added their own uncertainties to the game.

As the sun set in a red ball over the trees around the park lake, we would trail home, muddy, bruised and breathless, to Christmas tea with a luscious home-made cake, iced to look as though covered in icicles, with a bright red painted plaster Father Christmas on top. The grown-ups, meanwhile, had enjoyed a discussion of all the things they would rather we did not hear.

In the 1950s, winter was winter. Several Christmas holidays running there were heavy falls of snow between Christmas and New Year, delighting us with the transformed appearance of the High Street. The park lake froze over, making Breughel-like scenes of sporting prowess.

Gan-Gan, my mother's mother, always had a party at Christmas. Wearing a black velvet floor-length dress with gold embroidery on it, she welcomed cousins, aunts and uncles into her flat. We were always spoiled with two presents each from her, much appreciated of course. She hobbled with arthritis, smiled and called us "duckie" or "darling".

Ahead lay January and February, with their often cold and wet walks between home and school bus stop. But we'd had Christmases to remember all our lives, through the efforts of people who tried to make it special for us.

CHAPTER 12 – TOYS

The toys which mattered most to me for a long part of my childhood years were a doll's house and some farm animals and figures.

The doll's house wasn't new when I had it. It was in vaguely stockbroker's Tudor-style with six rooms. These were furnished with tiny pieces of furniture kept from my mother's neo-Georgian dolls house in her childhood. It occupied me for hours. I made little carpets for it and endlessly re-arranged all the rooms until I was completely satisfied.

Being short of bedroom space for the dolls' family, I asked my mother if the eldest daughter doll could share a bedroom with the uncle doll, a fetching little miniature in tweed trousers and a dark jacket. "Well, not really," she said, but would not elaborate.

Later, she gave me as a Christmas present; a 1950s dark brown varnished bedroom furniture suite. There was a double bed, a dressing table with a big mirror and a chest of three drawers. I was delighted. Then I got a 1950s kitchen set, all white paint, with fridge, sink and cooker. Now appearing antique, they entranced me.

The farm began with just a few animals added to as each birthday and Christmas came around.

I painted pieces of paper green and put the animals into green pastures.

There were all the usual pigs, chickens, cows, sheep and horses, made from brittle tin, or perhaps lead. There was even a land-girl figure, wearing breeches. The farmer's wife wore a long skirt with a white apron over it and carried a basket to collect the eggs. The farmer was dressed in a townie toy designer's idea of appropriate gear: gaiters, waistcoat, and tweed jacket. This was my earliest contact with what town-dwellers thought of fondly as "the rural idyll".

Because of the material from which they were made, the animals had an annoying tendency to snap their legs. I had to find ways of propping up three-legged animals with matchsticks and glue.

Then I was given a set of huntsmen and women. The pink coats and women riding side-saddle on elegant Arab-looking mounts gave me a whole new group to set up. A pack of black and white hounds, some of whose noses were on the ground following a scent, came with the horses. The hounds' legs broke even more easily, being only the thickness of a thin wire.

But I was happy with them. While the doll's house represented a still-unconscious desire for a home and children of my own, the farm represented the longing of the town or suburb dweller to live in the country. That desire became more and more insistent as I grew up.

The idea that a house could be a work of art, not only as architecture but also in terms of its contents, wasn't one I was aware of at that stage. But I could see that there would be pleasure to be gained from making choices about colours and fabrics in rooms, or this sofa rather than that one.

I had two dolls. One, Brownie, was a fabric doll with plasticized fabric face and brown hair and eyes. I was so attached to her that when I felt I'd got too old for dolls, I couldn't give or throw her away. She remains in the bottom drawer of the tallboy.

The other, Cathy, was a modern plastic baby doll. I used to cradle her and imagine she really was my baby. She was chubby and baby-like; Brownie was thinner and somehow more aloof. But Cathy was given away with her wardrobe of knitted baby clothes.

Some of my female friends developed a passion for roller skates, but this was one activity in which I could not join. When a friend lent me hers to try, I lacked the confidence to do as she did and zoom away along the pavement of Bessborough Road.

Instead, I clung pathetically to railings, gates and fences, the huge weight of the skates pulling down my feet, which slithered beyond my control. She, far more athletic and fearless than I, performed all the feats, leaving me with a very clear idea of my sporting limitations.

CHAPTER 13 – ILLNESS and WELLNESS

Although we were vaccinated against smallpox as babies, there was no protection against any other childhood infectious diseases. It was our duty to catch measles, mumps, and chickenpox and, particularly as we were all girls, German measles before we were old enough for these diseases to have serious consequences.

The more unusual childhood diseases, like scarlet fever, diphtheria and whooping cough occasionally cropped up among our friends, giving them time off school, for which we were envious.

There was no protection at all against meningitis. Until we were in our teens, when the Salk vaccine for polio became widely used, there was nothing against poliomyelitis.

We were told firmly by our parents that we must have this new, miraculous, preventive treatment. Out of my total ignorance, I rebelled. I should have been made to read literature describing the consequences of the disease. But I agreed in the end.

Today, I still come across people of my own generation, or older, who were stricken by this illness, just before protection became available. They have leg braces and walking sticks, and many physical tasks are a struggle for them. It was said that people picked up the disease at swimming pools.

Of other diseases, there were children who got leukaemia, and fewer of them survived than do today.

When one of our friends broke his or her arm climbing trees or playing cricket, we were envious. These people got lots of attention and a plaster cast for all their cronies to write messages upon. Appendicitis created a great stir and children were spoken of, by one mother to another, as being "rushed to hospital". In these terms, I felt our lives were a shade uneventful, as none of us ever broke even a finger.

We didn't have anorexia or bulimia. The hungry years of food shortages and the greater amount of exercise (especially walking twice a day to and from school with lunch at home) meant that, on the contrary, we were really hungry for meals.

We didn't cut ourselves, or only by accident. The epidemic of self-harm we hear of now had not begun. We mostly did not take illegal drugs and only very rarely prescribed ones. Obesity was quite unusual, probably because people didn't get the car out to post a letter two hundred yards away.

In case this makes us sound ridiculously smug and our lives lacking incident, I must say that alcohol, for my generation, retained its age-old glamour that it has always had for young adults. Drinking was seen as immensely sophisticated and I recall a friend of no great age telling me that his idea of heaven was a gin and lime. Smoking, to which a majority of our parents were addicted,, was seen as sophisticated by boys, but far less so by girls. By 1952, when the report of the Royal College of Surgeons made it clear that smoking was actually going to shorten your life, the tide began to turn.

I remember hearing that this or that person we knew socially had been promised a large bribe if they did not smoke till they were twenty-one. The theory was that if you could resist it until then, you were unlikely to take it up.

By the 1960s, I had two parents whose health was visibly affected by their smoking habits. It was also expensive and there were clearly better things on which to spend any cash one had managed to accumulate.

Some treatments were still quite primitive. For some years, I suffered from agonising boils on my shoulders. The cure for this was eating raw yeast. My mother tried to persuade me to eat this revolting substance, but I found it impossible. Eventually, she said, "If I go out of the room, will you eat it?" I said yes, but hid the smelly crumbs. Of course, she found them and said, "You've deceived me," very sadly. I felt sad about it, of course, and this episode made me all too conscious of my moral inadequacy.

Looking back, maybe more fruit and salads would have been better as a cure. My boils went on, one

97

succeeding another. They may even have been caused by an allergy to nickel in my bra straps. They were never regarded as important enough to need a specialist's advice.

I am old enough to remember the days when the word "cancer" was avoided in conversation. How this extraordinary taboo arose, I cannot imagine. In the more open talk of today, such an inhibition seems absurd.

Plastic surgery in those days was mainly for people who'd been burnt in aircraft crashes in the war, or who had disfiguring birthmarks. There was no notion of it being used to enlarge or reduce one's body, and there was no rush to get face-lifts. It was accepted that one grew older and one's appearance changed. People had lower expectations about how much of what one was born with could be altered.

CHAPTER 14 – THE HARROW IN WHICH WE GREW UP

From 1946, when I was three, we lived in a large house called Bradbys, on the High Street of Harrow-on-the-Hill.

The house was large because, besides my sisters, my parents and myself, it housed fifty adolescent boys aged thirteen to eighteen, who were in my father's care. More than half the house was boys' accommodation; there was a "boys' side" and a "private side" where we lived, and where the maids who cleaned the house slept on the top floor.

Along the High Street was a jumble of high Victorian and Georgian houses and the original Tudor building of the first Harrow School. There were Edwardian and neo-Georgian buildings too, and a lot of gardens, trees, terraces and open spaces.

The hill was separated from the teeming life of the suburbs, which surrounded it, by a belt of fields and woods. Some of them, like beautiful Church Fields, have since been built over.

The many fine trees which crowned the hilltop, increased the impression of height and even caused a resemblance to an Italian hill-town. The hill wasn't really very high but stood out distinctly from the flat lands of Northwick Park, Kenton, North Harrow and Rayner's Lane.

These fields, in some of which one could roam, also perhaps insulated the life of the school on the hill from the life of the community below. Only ten miles from Marble Arch, these previously undeveloped areas, with their grass, trees and views over North London were the scene of my earliest explorations.

Bradbys had an imposing porch with two carved stone eagles on top of it. The house was built in brown brick and had a black front door with a polished brass letterbox. My sister, Joanna, had a small room overlooking the eagles and looked out from her net-curtained window over the High Street.

I slept, to begin with, in the room called my father's dressing room. It had a big chest of drawers, with a mirror, a wardrobe with his suits in and a curtained alcove, with his shoes in rows below it.

When I looked from my bed in the dusk and when my mother thought I was going to sleep, I terrified myself by imagining that an intruder was standing behind those curtains and that his feet were in one of those pairs of shoes. He was poised to jump out and murder me.

This recurrent fear could not be dispelled. Getting out of bed and poking the curtains proved there was no one there — for the moment. But the next night, the fear returned.

I can't remember ever confiding my fear to anyone. Perhaps this was because of the equal fear of being thought silly.

My window looked onto the garden where a huge silver birch and slightly lower chestnut tree revealed the seasons to me. Beyond them lay a sea of semis, houses right as far as the horizon.

My very earliest memory of Bradbys was of being given a scooter when we first moved there. Joanna, three years older, had a fairy cycle, a modest two-wheeled affair. Stabilisers hadn't been invented.

My next really vivid memory is of the smell of azaleas. There was a bed with three really well-grown specimens; yellow, orange and salmon pink. Now, whenever I have a breath of this heady scent, I am back, a child, dwarfed by the big, spreading bushes, entranced equally by colour and aroma.

We also had a bank of bluebells and a border with philadelphus, Solomon's seal and forsythia.

Below this, beyond the grass tennis court where the boys played on summer evenings, there was a large ancient pear tree, covered in hundreds of bronze-coloured pears, and something we called "Treasure Wood".

This was a small area closely planted with trees and shrubs. We made houses there, with half-bricks, lumps of stone and sticks. We buried dead baby birds and indulged in let's pretend and mothers' and fathers' games.

The ritual of burying the birds somehow helped to make up for the sadness of their deaths. In these small ceremonies, we acted out, unknowingly, the emotions and actions we would display later on when people who'd been important in our lives died.

There was a large rockery, rather neglected, between the upper, sloping part of the garden and the tennis court. One day, I found a fritillary growing there, many miles from its natural habitat. It was a source of wonder; that so slender stem and the dappled bi-colour surface of the petals.

Below all this was the kitchen garden, ruled over by somebody called Mr Willoughby. Vegetables grew there and there was a small red brick cottage where one of our cooks lived for a while.

At the very bottom stood a cherry tree. Under the thickly clustered white flowers, I took my very first photograph. Pointing the camera at the canopy of blossom, towards the vivid blue sky visible between the laden twigs, I yearned to record this dazzling sight.

But when the tiny picture was fetched from the chemist with the other pictures from the film, there was only the vaguest black-and-white resemblance to what I'd seen. It was an early lesson in the gap between an astonishing sight and the rendering of it in paint or film.

The garden struck one as being a very peculiar shape. It was very narrow at one point and quite wide at others. It was as though all the surrounding gardens had taken their territory from it. All manner of brick and stone walls, rickety fences and scrubby hedges edged it, as though these had been put up piecemeal at different times.

It wasn't an elegant garden at all, but in it, I learned to love all my future gardens.

Inside the house, my parents perpetuated the standards of the Edwardian and Neo-Georgian eras in which they had been brought up.

We had a night nursery for my sister, Gillian, to sleep in and a day nursery for day times.

A series of "mothers helps" as they were known was employed to look after us, when my parents were preoccupied with school life. There were two Dutch girls, very homesick. I think their time with us was brief. Once my sister, Gillian, started school, my mother managed us on her own.

It was a tradition at Harrow that every boy had his own room and did not sleep communally in dormitories, as at other boarding schools. These tiny cells had a bed folded vertically against the wall, a desk, a window, a chair and not much else.

We girls, who saw these rooms occasionally in the holidays, thought them very spartan. Perhaps their austerity made the boys appreciate their homes.

The austere surroundings had another virtue; there was little in them which could be destroyed.

My parents put an immense amount of time, thought and energy into the welfare of their fifty male teenagers.

Once, I overheard them discussing the problems and prospects of a particular boy, who had been making difficulties.

"Of course," my mother said, "the trouble with that family is that they just have too much money".

I was puzzled. How on earth could one ever have too much money? What complications could flow from being in that state? I couldn't make sense of it.

Once, when the fees went up to £500 a year, I heard my father declaring that the parents would never stand for it. Now that the fees are around £42,000 a year it all seems so long ago.

Those who worked at the school and their neighbours who lived on the hill but commuted to London for work, formed a striking community. The people who composed it were not invariably like-minded but made up a group who had at least some common values. The conservatism of some was already being challenged in the late 1950s by newcomers. The view that the boys were being educated to become an elite who would go out and rule the empire had to give way, if only because that empire itself was dissolving.

At Harrow School, one got no training to be a house master. For that matter, no teacher training was required either, merely that aspiring staff members had a degree and a desire to teach. Managing fifty boys, with all their associated adolescent problems, a variable number of live-in staff, and one's own family as well as teaching in the classroom was a formidable lifestyle.

Supplying everything needed on a tight budget was really difficult. My father tried various ways of managing better. He kept poultry for eggs and meat and warned us to stay out of the way when Mr Willoughby was slaughtering them for an end-of-term feast called House Supper. He tried to grow vegetables on another house master's spare land but was defeated in this cause by the overwhelming growth of summer weeds which he lacked the time to pull up.

My ignorance of the cultural wealth of Harrow was complete. I never knew that the artist and author David Jones had actually been a resident, nor did I know that Trollope's parents lived there, or about the thousand years of history of St. Mary's church.

As a child, it did not occur to me that the Harrow I knew could change. But after leaving for good when I married at twenty-two, I didn't return for some years. When I finally paid a visit there, I was shocked.

The immense changes wrought by "progress" in the Greater Harrow area between 1950 and 2000 were summed up for me by one location, unrecognisable on my return.

Coming from the centre of London by the Metropolitan line, you emerged from it at Harrow-on-the-Hill station. You descended a flight of stairs, where the unique tube smell still seemed to linger, and came out into the open.

When I was a child, at that point you saw and smelled flowers. Webbs, a florist, lay on your left, and dozens of buckets held bunches of flowers whose colour drew your eye. It was also a nursery garden and sold plants. As you inhaled their scent you seemed to have forgotten the dirty smell of the city and its transport system, of people crowded together and polluted air. This flower shop seemed to symbolise the freshness and cleanness of suburbia, as opposed to the filth of the metropolis.

Of course, the kinds of flowers varied according to the season. Sometimes pot plants, especially shocking-pink cyclamen, sometimes a great mass of daffodils, sometimes a glorious rainbow of chrysanthemums; the smell of these made one want to grasp bunches of them and run away. It was the last trace of a pastoral Harrow which existed before Metro-land first became developed.

But when I returned years later, it had all been swept away. A big concrete bus station and a shopping centre, anonymous and soulless, were in its place. Either of these structures could have been anywhere. Their dreariness was no substitute for the flowers which had awaited the weary commuter, shopper or schoolgirl.

Where, I wondered, had Heathfield School gone? Where was Dorothy Perkins, whose windows I had sometimes yearned over, and where the chemist, whose lighted plate glass had displayed all manner of covetable cosmetics?

There had been a furniture store too, with whole room areas laid out in the big windows with "G-plan" furniture. As a girl, I had often gazed at these, daydreaming of a house of my own, to arrange as I liked.

Now, it has all gone.

On the hill itself, the different buildings gradually became more familiar to me.

The school chapel, a building designed to resemble the Sainte Chapelle in Paris, was a place we sometimes accompanied my mother to on Sunday evenings.

All along the inside walls were memorial tablets recording the deaths of young old Harrovians on a foreign field. These plaques of marble, of many colours, and of alabaster, recorded so many tragedies. Collectively, they expressed the agony of a whole era, a loss which was burnt into my consciousness.

Over the road from the chapel, was the large building put up to honour Harrow's war dead. In front of that, a high flight of white steps stood. Next to the chapel was the Vaughan Library, with coloured brickwork and a magnolia on each of the lawns in front of it. Above was the red brick Tudor building, the Old Schools.

Down a slope, below this landmark structure, in an area dedicated to PE, was the school's gym. My father made frequent visits here on Saturday and to the fives and squash courts nearby, and I attended social events, like Scottish dancing as a teenager in the big echoing spaces of the gym.

Round the walls of the gym were carved or painted the words, "I have finished the work thou gavest me to do." This sentence struck me when I first saw it and haunted me all my life. I only discovered very recently that it came from the so-called "Prayer of Jesus" in St. John's Gospel, chapter 17. I think the gym walls also said, "Whatsoever thy hand findest to do, do it with thy might."

At some point, I found out that the gym had been built in memory of the brief lives of boys slaughtered in the First World War. The notion that anyone could have completed their lives by eighteen, nineteen, twenty or any age we would regard as very young, was hard to accept. Could it be true?

The other quotation about doing things with all your might stayed in my mind as an ideal, one which I didn't often live up to. Carelessness, sloppiness and doing things by halves were more my style.

My father would take us on several trips on Saturdays to watch "his" boys in various kinds of exercise. We trotted behind his giant strides trying to keep up. Boys swarmed past in a complex range of garbs, with different caps, scarves, blazers and shirts denoting their team or house. For years, we were taken to rugger matches in the autumn term, Harrow football in the Easter term and cricket matches in the summer term. We ought to have become experts in the finer points of these games, but we never did. Our hearts were not in it.

Watching the cricket was more enjoyable than the other two sports. We sat in the sun on wooden seats at the edge of a flawless sweep of grass, on which white-clad figures ran, hurled balls, hit sixes and caught people out. Bus drivers drove slowly past to watch as their vehicles ran along Bessborough Road. It was a great meeting place for masters, their wives and local cricket fanciers. The chestnut-tree-lined track of cinders which led down to the Sixth Form ground from Middle Road was dark and shadowy in summer, a tunnel of shade from which one came blinking into the sunlight.

Before our eyes passed a performance of athletic prowess. It seemed, in the trance in which we watched, that this pattern of summer and winter spectator sport would never end.

My father used to be desperately sorry when his house, playing against another house, was defeated. He couldn't, or wouldn't express to us his feelings of disappointment. Every housemaster wanted his house to be the best, most successful and most deserving of glory.

As we grew towards our teens, individual boys became the objects of our attention, as our parents must have known they would. From a distance, we admired looks and learned reputations. As people have from the beginning of time, we invested boys with all kinds of virtues they may never have possessed.

My elder sister, Joanna, exchanged with a friend minutely detailed accounts of sightings of boys who attracted them. It was all very decorous. From afar, we fantasised about them.

When I grew a little older, I was given a room of my own, the old day nursery. Gillian had started school now and there was no further need of a nursery for her. She had her own room too.

The room I was given faced the garden. It was freshly papered for me; peach with white spots. I had a bed with a blue cotton bedspread, an electric fire to dry my hair by when it was washed, a desk, a wardrobe — and a view. Being on the second floor, I could see the sunset every night, over Middlesex. Behind the birch tree and the chestnut, the colours built up to a climax of brilliance and then faded into darkness. I never tired of gazing at them.

In the distance, a big gasometer in South Harrow hid the new airport at Heathrow. On the horison, leafy Pinner lay. The other hamlets of Middlesex lay under rows and rows of terraces and semis.

When my father first moved to Harrow, he'd walked across fields to see his mother in Ruislip. That was 1933. Now, arterial roads and suburban closes covered up what had been those pastures. I learned to wonder what it all could have been like, before the twentieth century. Tube lines and bus routes replaced the quiet lanes. Something in my mind craved a rural landscape and existence.

For daily shopping, we had an International Stores, Mash's the greengrocer, a haberdashers, an electrical shop, post office, shoe mender, bookshop and chemist. For all other shopping, one had to descend from the Hill into Harrow itself.

In the International Stores, you stood in front of a scarred and pitted wooden counter darkened with age. In front of it was a whole row of large biscuit tins. From these, the amount you wanted was weighed out. No plastic packets, no self-service. Sugar came in dark blue strong paper bags. Bacon was sliced by a machine freshly for each customer, not sold entombed in plastic.

The lady behind the counter knew my mother by name and the transaction included some conversation. My mother also frequently encountered friends in the shop, on the pavement or on the walk to and from home. Food shopping was a social activity, as well as exercise, carried out unhurriedly, and a welcome chance to leave the house.

Not many of the wives she knew were employed, so shopping was not a rushed business squashed into the lunch hour. There was time to admire a new baby, ask after an ageing parent or discuss how someone's daughter was getting on at her new school. Given this setting, gossip and news flowed in a never-ending circulation. My mother believed she was always busy, but it was a leisurely life compared with the working mothers today.

One vanished occupation was that of rag and bone man. In addition to the horse and cart which delivered the milk, we used to see regularly the shabby cart he used, pulled by a dejected-looking horse. His cry, which I could not for years decipher, echoed through the neighbourhood. He would collect pretty well anything no longer wanted, an early form of recycling.

Now his role has been taken over by car boot sales and landfill.

Other street characters were classed by my parents as "hooligans" or "Teddy Boys". Hooligans shouted, ate in the street, (both offences in my parents' eyes), or went in for minor acts of vandalism. "Teddy Boys" dressed elaborately in Edwardian clothes and "showed off", also a sin. Sometimes they shouted at boys inside my father's house, hoping to provoke them into retaliation. Our boys were sternly instructed to keep away from the windows.

The sound background of the 1950s was very different from that of the early twenty-first century. There was far less aeroplane traffic in the London area than there is now, and we never saw or heard helicopters. Although the infant Heathrow airport was only a few miles off, our suburb did not lie under its flight path. Gatwick was not yet open. Northolt Aerodrome was close, but we were not conscious of much disturbance from it.

There was no TV noise. Our domestic listening centred around the wireless and Joanna's piano-playing.

Later, she became addicted to the Top Ten and Radio Luxembourg, so we sometimes overheard bits of those.

My father finally changed his mind about television after hiring one for the Coronation in 1953. After some initial suspicion (lent greater weight by the view that no good could come from something whose name had a Greek prefix and a Latin suffix), he bought one.

We children quickly discovered that we could justify watching any programme if it could be labelled "educational".

Other sounds were heard in Harrow more easily than in other parts of Middlesex which had been more comprehensively built over.

There were still a great many large gardens in the Harrow-on-the-Hill I remember. These contained forest-sized trees of beech, chestnut and oak, as well as the usual suburban lilacs, pink cherries, laburnum and fruit trees. So, the first sound you heard on waking was that of birds singing.

Later on, some of the big gardens had blocks of apartments built on them. Owners of others sold off a slice of the garden for a new single dwelling to be built. Gradually, there were fewer trees and fewer birds.

Beyond the sound of the birds, a low roar, which I couldn't at first identify, went on the whole day. When I asked what it was, I was told it was the sound of London traffic. We were ten miles from Marble Arch.

On going into the country, which I always felt was my biggest treat, the first thing I noticed was the absence of that roar. In those pre-motorway days, the area beyond Middlesex sounded quiet.

When my father took us to Chorleywood Common, our nearest countryside, we were away from the non-stop rumble of city traffic. Today, on the Chilterns, one may well be disturbed by aeroplanes landing at or taking off from Luton Airport.

Then there were sounds of bells chiming; the school day at Harrow was punctuated by these. We also heard the bells of St. Mary's Church.

The boys in my parents' care made their own contribution to background noise. From their blocks of rooms and staircases came the sounds of pounding feet, laughter, shouts, and the summons, "Boy!" when monitors called junior boys to carry out menial tasks for them. A feudal system reigned. Summary punishments were heralded by the same piercing shout. I was too young to question the justice of the system.

The telephone rang a great deal: other masters to talk about boys, parents of boys to talk about boys and master's wives making social arrangements.

In summer, open windows brought us other sounds: tennis racquets pinging on the ball, the thwack of a cricket bat hitting a six to the boundary, louder church and chapel bells and the tramp of feet between lessons in the High Street, accompanied by much chattering.

The houses of masters and the school's many historic buildings were looked after by a team of people collectively known as The Works Department. The never-ending jobs of maintaining these Tudor, Georgian and Victorian structures meant that hammering was often to be heard. Usually, one or other building was in scaffolding. It was said that houses like Bradbys, underneath which the slope of the hill fell away, were permanently crumbling. Dry rot cropped up too and was spoken about in awed tones.

My mother craved the redecoration of rooms. "Leave it to me, Mrs Thompson", the clerk of the Works would cry. She did, but it always took a very long time to get anything done.

The great DIY revolution had not begun. It would not have occurred to my mother that she could paint a room.

The Harrow in which we grew up was only one of the dozens of suburban areas around London itself.

When we left it, perhaps to visit our several relations whose address was followed by an initial or two and a number to indicate that they really dwelt in London itself, we entered a very different setting.

There were sudden gaps in terraces of buildings left by the Blitz. For several years after the war ended these spaces were a feature of the cityscape.

Knowing little then of the bloodshed of the war, we were chiefly aware of the events of 1939-45 as the means by which London had been damaged. One would see a fireplace two floors up, still embedded in a wall, with the sky above and random heaps of broken bricks below. Fragments of wallpaper showing the colour schemes of rooms still hung there. Windows empty of glass looked onto derelict gardens massively overgrown with brambles amid the heaps of rubble. Willowherb and buddleia rapidly colonised these sites.

Shortages of building materials were one reason why the spaces between buildings lasted so long after hostilities were over. Builders had been called up into the army, Britain itself was broke after 1935 and there was a lack of money to invest in rebuilding too.

We were familiar with prefabs. There were estates of them all over the place, put up quickly to house people who'd been made homeless by the Blitz. They were intended to last only a few years, but some were still used forty years after the war ended. They looked compact and basic, but no doubt were heaven to people who'd had to cram into shared accommodation with their parents or children after the trauma of their home being destroyed. Sixty thousand of them were built.

In the late 1950s and early 1960s, huge new concrete department stores went up on Oxford Street. My mother deplored the demolition of Marshall and Snelgrove, her favourite big shop.

It was unique in having windows with daylight coming in on all floors. She maintained that daylight was vital to assess the true colour of a garment before buying it. To the end of her life, she deplored the modern arrangement of everything being lit artificially.

Districts like St. John's Wood changed too. The large houses in immense, shady gardens became flats.

The gardens themselves were sold off as building sites. Quiet backwaters of London became frenzied with builders' noise, scaffolding, lorries, clumps of materials and garish signs.

The human scale of pre-twentieth century London was disappearing. Land being costly, developers went for the tallest buildings they were allowed. Wren's London was overshadowed by giant structures. Just as seriously, neighbourly terraces were destroyed and their inhabitants were put into high-rise blocks of flats. This was our new, post-war London.

CHAPTER 15 -ROUTINE

I opened my eyes to the sound of my mother making early morning tea in my parents' room next door to where I slept.

Next, I would hear a rustling sound as she dug in a cupboard above my bed for biscuits to help her last out until breakfast time.

Getting dressed was next. My uniformless dame school meant that we went to school in our ordinary clothes. I envied people who had a blazer; this showed that they were part of an in-group.

Later, when I had reached secondary school and been compelled to wear its uniform, I longed for the individuality of mufti. Instead of yearning to be part of a group, I wanted to break free and be an individual, wearing my own choice of clothes.

Once we were judged to be able to cross roads safely, we walked to school alone. The mass hysteria about paedophiles lay far into the future.

These walks did not just make us active. They gave us a chance to observe the weather, birds, flowers, and especially the flowering shrubs for which suburbs have always been famous. The changing seasons encountered first hand, not from the back of cars as spectators. Neighbours whom we knew, greeted us en route and reinforced the idea that we were living in a neighbourhood.

Every morning at breakfast, my father had all the news pages of the Times. My mother had the two centre pages, which had readers' letters and editorials. This pattern never varied; my mother read the news pages later.

We also took the Evening Standard, which dropped through the letterbox during the afternoon. I got very addicted to this paper, but when I was seven, my parents gave up taking it because I kept asking them things like what a co-respondent was. In another age, my questions would probably have been answered. As it was, my parents thought it best to remove such worldly subjects from my mind.

When breakfast was over, my parents separated to their various duties. My father put on a mortarboard and academic gown and went to his classroom. My mother went to talk to the cooks.

On Mondays, this meant a lengthy meeting called "doing the menus" when it was decided what all the occupants of the house would eat for the next week. There was great anxiety about providing variety and nutrition while having to stay within a budget.

At eleven a.m., my parents forgathered in my father's study for something called Morning Tea. During this, cigarette smoke hung in the air as they sipped tea. My mother had another glance at the paper, my father saw boys with requests. Passive smoking was our lot for years.

After that, they both hurried off to resume work. My mother had to check on whether the maids were doing their jobs properly. She also had to order large quantities of food from different wholesalers, in order never to run out.

When they'd eaten lunch with the fifty boys and matron, my parents frequently felt obliged to watch football and cricket matches in order to support "their boys".

At some point in the day, my father must have found time to mark boys' work, go to staff meetings, teach lessons, see parents, and act as host to Old Harrovians who often visited with wife or girlfriend in tow.

After supper, my father toured the house, presumably checking up that the boys were working at their prep and not bullying each other. When he returned from that, the official day was over.

As far as the children were concerned, there was a strict system of bedtimes, according to age. Being allowed to stay up to grown-ups' supper, which for some years Joanna was allowed to do, but I too young, was seen as the ultimate privilege.

For years, I went to sleep to the sound of Joanna doing her piano practice. The piano was in the hall and all its sound echoed up the stairs towards my room.

Gillian, being nearly four years younger than I was, would already have been asleep.

First, there were the scales, with the sounds of notes rippling up and down from high to low and back again.

Then came the actual pieces. On summer evenings, when with the light coming through my curtains and the noise of people who were still very much awake echoing through the air, it was hard to sleep anyway.

When the sounds of Beethoven reached me, I found myself really listening.

In the parquet-floored hall, with the gleaming mahogany tallboy and the extra-wide doormat behind our immense front door, she dutifully carried out the stipulated practice time.

Behind her were the windows onto the street, with strange panes that prevented anyone from seeing in. There was also one of several doors which led to the boys' side of the house.

How did the music flow out of someone's fingers like that? How did that person interpret the mysterious markings on the sheet of music, a secret language as impenetrable to me as the words on the blackboard had been before I could read?

When she shut the piano lid, our side of the house became quiet.

But in that time of listening, my musical tastes had been formed forever.

Now, in my retirement years, when I hear the same music played on the radio by, say, Alfred Brendel, I am no more impressed than I was when I heard Joanna play them. Not because his playing isn't better — of course it is — but when she played it, that was when I heard it first.

Sunday was really different from the other six days in the 1940s and 1950s.

No shops at all opened on Sundays and all small shops were also shut on Wednesday afternoons. Shop workers thus managed at least one complete day of rest with their families. No one expected such employees to give up the only day in the week traditionally devoted to family life to the pursuit of profit.

As a result, the streets were quiet. It was a pause in the business of earning a living, a rest from commuting and an absence of spending. People ate a large ritual lunch or dinner, did gardening, walked their children, read newspapers, slept late or went to church according to their habits.

On Saturdays, people made sure they had in the house everything needed to last until the shops opened again on Mondays. Nobody considered it a hardship that you could not go shopping seven days a week.

From quite a young age, I and my sisters were sent to Sunday School.

This took place in the drawing room of the Harrow School Chaplain and his wife.

She was childless and masters' children were invited to learn from her what Christianity was about.

Rows of cushions and footstools were set along the floor for us to sit on, according to size. We had coloured stickers to put into books, showing events from the Bible. We were told the parables and the miracles wrought by Jesus. I vividly remember hearing from her about the crucifixion of Jesus.

When we were considered old enough, we were allowed to graduate to go to the Parish Church but permitted to exit before the sermon. It was thought we might if we stayed, find the service too long. However, the sermon was the only part of the service expressed in contemporary English and one could just as well have come only for the sermon.

Services then were nearly always the Book of Common Prayer ones and lessons were read from the King James Bible. This early grounding in the magnificent language of the seventeenth century was one of the aspects of my education that I most valued in the years to come. Before the prosaic New English Bible came into use, you could be confident of entering any church and hearing the extraordinary poetry of the Authorized Version. The familiar passages were repeated in an annual cycle so that we knew many by heart.

Our material lives were dominated by the names of products which today are unheard of. Bakelite, not plastic, made our radios, called wirelesses. Rayon, not nylon, many of our clothes. If one was cleaning the bath, one used Vim — Latin for strength, power and force.

Unwanted insects were slaughtered by squirting a Flit gun at them. If we were thought to need a tonic, we were given something called Radio Malt, a sticky, syrup-like substance supposedly crammed with trace elements which would cure our ills. During and after the war, children were entitled to bottles of sweetened concentrated orange juice, cod-liver oil and a ration of milk. Strange products like National Dried Milk, in a big tin, and dried egg were supposed to be adequate substitutes for the real thing.

We hadn't heard of duvets. Beds were made with cotton, linen or flannelette sheets, wool blankets on top of these, and then a slippery, satin-covered eiderdown, stuffed with real duck feathers and very warm and lightweight. Sometimes there was a bedspread covering the whole ensemble. The first domestic chore we were expected to learn was how to make our own beds; there was to be no leaving this and going off to school without bothering to do it. Not to have done this would have been sloppy. And as for people who did not strip their beds to air them, they were unspeakable.

In the depths of winter, or if you were ill in bed, you might qualify for a hot water bottle. Electric blankets were looked upon as a dangerous innovation. On cold nights, one's feet were thrust down into an icy cold bed. One had to wriggle vigorously to create enough warmth to be able to sleep.

CHAPTER 16 – AMUSEMENTS and OCCUPATIONS

"But what did you do when there was no television?"

Children home from school, or enjoying the holidays which seem long to adults but which for children can never be long enough, played a lot of indoor games. Not just the ones which needed a large number of people to play, like charades and murder in the dark, but paper and board games: ludo, consequences, snakes and ladders, Monopoly and Scrabble.

Although these games were ostensibly amusements, some of them involved a lot of counting, spelling and multiplication, so they did increase our mental agility.

Some children played instruments, piano or violin mainly, but the guitar was just beginning its meteoric rise in popularity.

They collected things: stamps, cigarette cards, rock samples, birds' eggs, butterflies and autographs. At that time, it was not illegal to raid nature; it was thought that her bounty was limitless.

They wrote diaries and letters. My sister, Joanna, carried on an extremely detailed correspondence with a friend who lived only four hundred yards away and whom she saw very frequently.

Some belonged to Scouts, Guides, Cubs or Brownies, delighting in dressing up in yet another uniform and mastering various skills.

Then there was sewing. As niece to two aunts who were virtuoso patchwork people, I got plenty of encouragement. From my small pocket money, I saved for a square of felt at the haberdashers, which could be made into dolls' house carpets, or presents for grown-ups. I graduated from that with an intense interest in materials of all sorts, ancient and modern, and thence to how clothes were made.

Glitterwax was a substance we all enjoyed making things from. One had to melt it first and this we did on the metal fireguard bars in front of the nursery's electric fire. When it was soft enough, models could be made from it, but it was necessary to work quickly before it went hard again.

It was not popular with grown-ups. Small bits of it got onto carpets or were forgotten on the fireguard and dripped down liquidly to the floor.

Both my sisters learned to knit, but I never. Was I too impatient to keep trying?

We did occasionally go to the cinema, but hardly ever. The films we saw were ones selected for the boys at Harrow, shown three times a term. We were thus spared Hollywood versions of great pieces of literature which dominated the cinema of the 30s and 40s. I remember being absolutely carried away by the realism of a film about a little girl, Mandy, born deaf and dumb, who learns to speak. The subject matter was my earliest introduction to the world of disability and a shocking lesson on how lucky I was to have all my faculties.

Telling my mother about it afterwards with huge enthusiasm, she damped me down by saying I wouldn't always feel so admiring about films. It captured my imagination and brought home to me the role of the teacher in giving a person without speech the power to communicate.

The forgotten boredom Philip Larkin described his childhood as struck a chord with me. Oh, the long afternoons of childhood, when one longed for teatime to break the monotony. Why was there boredom? Because I was a child and could not always decide how to spend my time. Because I didn't know enough about how to get deeply into a subject and occupy myself. Because, like most children, my attention span was short. And because I didn't realise that every day and hour was precious.

Wearing a pink dress with small flowers on, I remember being bored on a Sunday afternoon. Then we went for a walk and I fell into the swampy end of the park lake, going home a dripping mess.

Later, when I was judged old enough to walk to my first school alone, I amused myself finding variations on the route back to school after lunch. The most straightforward route was a short downhill walk. There were lots of other ways though: down Waldron Road and along Crown Street, down Roxeth Hill and up Middle Road, or even down West Street, along Bessborough Road and up from the Timber Carriage. This activity gave me pride in being an explorer, as well as feeling daring for being engaged in something the grown-ups didn't know about.

Children's Hour, on the radio, was the high spot of the day. It was a magic fifty-five minutes when I listened rapt to one drama, serial, nature talk or poetry anthology after another. Norman and Henry Bones, the boy detectives, Jennings and Darbyshire, two boys at a boarding school with delightfully comic masters, especially Mr Wilkins; I found it all completely enthralling.

It was on Children's Hour that I first heard the quotation "A green thought in a green shade", in a programme celebrating summer. The world of words, of different voices, themes and treatments of stories which I was already discovering in books, came across to me without the distraction of images.

The Archers too was a programme I became addicted to for a few years. I *had* to hear every episode. When ill and home from school I listened to Mrs Dale's Diary too, a saga of suburban existence whose details entirely escape me except that Mrs Dale's husband was a doctor called Jim.

Nowadays, these would be classed as "soaps" along with "EastEnders" and "Coronation Street". At that time, they were avidly followed by thousands of listeners. They nudged me towards the world of fiction, with all its important aspects: dialogue, plot, characterisation, setting and style. Fiction became for me as necessary as food, clothes and warmth. Entering fictional worlds became a major preoccupation.

Then there was Woman's Hour, which as I entered my teens beguiled many a school holiday afternoon. On it, I heard a phrase I couldn't interpret: "Women's Diseases". How could there be diseases which only women could catch? I couldn't work it out — to begin with.

Skipping ropes and hula-hoops were both crazes when I was primary school age. One had to have one, of course. The most athletic of my peers could do extraordinary things with their ropes: I could only goggle. Hoops, which in the nineteenth century had been used to bowl along, now gyrated around our bodies in strange patterns.

Both crazes kept us moving. Although "fitness" was valued to some extent, this had not become the fetish that it is now with some.

Giggling was a big part of our childhood. Hours of time were dominated by this simple form of enjoyment. We knew a family of three girls, roughly our ages, who lived in a white clapboard farmhouse down the hill. This building had miraculously survived into the twentieth century, near the school's cricket fields.

Many times, we went to play at their house. There was a lot of running up and down stairs, screaming with laughter. We giggled so much that our cheeks ached. Stevie, Julie and Rosanne, they were called, and I never knew what happened to them after we left our dame-school. Mass hysteria? Or just a normal phase in the maturation of the female?

Julie was the tearaway, the rebel who was always in trouble. Her dress was dirty, her hair wild. I almost envied her reputation. The six of us must have driven their and our parents mad.

A key destination for our outings was the local park. This had swings, slides, seats, a large grassy area with flowers — and a park-keeper.

This was a man in a peaked cap who kept order. He saw that people obviously aged over twelve did not go on the swings. Possibly he also broke up fights and prevented kidnaps, though we never saw him do this. We were in awe of him. I can't remember ever seeing graffiti on the shelter or vandalism on the play equipment, and maybe his presence prevented these.

There were big chestnut trees along one side of the park which protected it and separated it from the approach to the station on the other side. Their dense, deep green foliage cast a welcome shade in summer.

The walk home, inevitably uphill, tired us some more. It would never have been considered that we would go there by car; it was felt it was good for children to walk, a belief now being rediscovered.

No account of how we spent our out-of-school time as children would be complete without mentioning the hours day-dreaming absorbed.

A tendency to this appeared at awkward moments; if bored one could go off into a distant and impossible world in which one was beautiful, successful, brilliant and popular. One had a house, furnished with G-plan furniture, an immense garden and, of course, a horse to ride. In one's wardrobe would be dozens of breathtaking outfits for every conceivable occasion.

None of this happened to me. But the dreams mattered. As Einstein said, the imagination is more important than knowledge.

Later, the dreams were not materialistic. They were about being famous. Recognition for doing something really important began to matter. I didn't realise then that many were called, but few were chosen.

The only sport for which I felt any enthusiasm at all was swimming. I couldn't hit a ball, as I discovered humiliatingly at an open tennis competition, in which I came bottom.

But because Harrow possessed a really beautiful outdoor pool, I had all the opportunity I wanted to swim. We could go at weekends and in the summer holidays.

The pool lay across the football fields and on the far side of the Watford Road. It was L-shaped and surrounded by a thick belt of fine trees and shrubs which gave both shelter and privacy. The deepest water was where the two arms of the L met, and there were diving boards too.

Often with a friend, I did the buttercup-strewn walk over the fields and upon the concrete footbridge to Ducker. On a hot day, when one had already walked the best part of a mile, one was already very warm by this point.

Ripping off our clothes in the communal female changing room, we plunged into the water's coolness, rejoicing at the contrast.

Once I lay by the pool for what seemed like hours believing that I would effortlessly turn brown all over in no time. The only result was after I'd got home, embarrassingly red skin. Jumping in a large number of times and displacing rather a lot of water was enormous fun.

On visits to my grandmother at West Hill House, there were opportunities to admire the sun setting behind bare beeches at the bottom of Dr Tisdall's garden. This was a childish enthusiasm I never grew out of.

CHAPTER 17 – TRANSPORT and COMMUNICATIONS

Right through my childhood and teenage years, no bus ran up to the top of Harrow-on-the-Hill, although several routes plied around its base. One had to get off the big red London Transport bus from Canons Park, Edgware, where my secondary school was, and walk about a mile uphill and then along the High Street.

This could be quite an enjoyable walk, but when tired at the end of a North London Collegiate School day, caused me to reach home drained of energy.

And yet, those walks with their twice-daily opportunities to observe seasons, trees and architecture had their advantages. They gave one thinking time between the mental input at school and the interchanges of family life at home. They laid the foundations of future fitness too.

En route to or from the bus stop, one met friends and neighbours. This reinforced our belief that we were living in a community whose members recognised each other and said something appropriate.

I had no idea at that time how, fifty years later, sought after this ideal of a community would become.

In the "village" atmosphere of Harrow-on-the-Hill, concern for neighbours was in evidence because we all knew each other.

When the high-rise blocks started to go up in cities in the 1960s, communities whose occupants all knew each other, began to be destroyed. To know and be known seemed normal and natural because that was all we had ever experienced.

There were tube lines leading into central London; the same lines if you went in the opposite direction, took you to what was known as "London's Countryside". This meant the Chilterns; other lines went to seductive places like Kew, Richmond Park, Osterley and Wimbledon Common. Commuting was largely done by tube; people kept their cars for longer journeys.

The big London termini, from which you could travel by train to all distant parts of Britain, were immense and impressive structures. The Euston Arch, a superb piece of splendid construction, was demolished by philistines in the 1960s. The hotel of red brick and gothic ornament at St. Pancras remains.

These echoing, often dirty, big stations were romantic because of the places you could get to from them.

Communications were very different from today. No mobile phones or text messages, no e-mail and no faxes.

But there were telegrams when a person needed to know something quickly and could not be reached by phone. There were people who had no phone. Telegrams had been used to inform relations of deaths in wartime. By the time I was a young woman, they were mainly kept for greeting purposes. If you got married or had a baby, the telegrams, gaily decorated, flooded in.

Telephone calls were made using a four-digit number preceded by the first three letters of the name of the exchange. Harrow-on-the-Hill was BRY for Byron on the exchange; Kenton was WORdsworth. There was none of having to remember or look up an eleven-digit number, as there is today. Outside big cities, the exchange name was of the town or village itself.

When we embarked on solo journeys to London by tube, we were exhorted always to have on us four old pennies — big heavy copper things — with which to telephone home if we got stranded, or for a lift back from the station by my father if it was after dark.

Phoning foreign countries, like visiting them, was regarded as impossibly exotic. One wrote then waited a while for a reply. Lots of families had someone in Australia, New Zealand, East or South Africa, or Canada. Big collections of foreign stamps were easily amassed.

We had two deliveries of post every day except Sunday. In my paternal grandmother's youth, in the first decade of the twentieth century, she told me that one could send a letter in the morning and receive a reply to it the same evening. Evening deliveries disappeared before I was born.

How cheap the post was then; three old pence, about one new penny, for anywhere in Britain. One never heard of items going astray in the post, as they so often seem to today. One certainly never read in the papers of half a million items of post getting lost every year.

Driving around the country was rather more of an adventure than in the twenty-first century, although not as much of an adventure as in the days before the driving test was invented.

If a driver belonged, as my father did, to the RAC, then he or she had a blue and white logo fixed to the front of the car. When an RAC patrolman, on his motorcycle, was riding past you in the opposite direction, he always saluted. The hand, clad in a special large gauntlet, then dropped back to grip the handlebars.

CHAPTER 18 – WEATHER, SEASONS, FOG and SMOG

In the early 1950s, global warming hadn't been heard of. Winters were cold and we frequently had snow at Christmas or just after. This, of course, was most especially prized when it fell in the holidays. We had tobogganing on the park fields, which sloped steeply.

For three or four winters running, the park lake froze over. Boys besieged my father's study, asking him to sign chits for them to have skates supplied and put on their parents' bills.

I was enchanted by the sight of the High Street blanketed in white, with no tyre marks to spoil the brilliance. When we woke to snow, we saw roofs hidden by dazzling white, making the sky look dirty.

At school, we had Robert Bridges' poem "London Snow", that perfect evocation of snow in the city.

Thaws were mourned.

Summer, on the other hand, was often what my mother called a "washout". Rain poured relentlessly onto dozens of cricket matches in May and June, making the British summer the butt of international jokes.

But the big weather hazard when I was growing up was smog. This was generated by atmospheric pollution from factories and domestic fires and mixed with fog. Before the clean air acts, we had it every winter. If people had lung problems it could be very dangerous for them and there were deaths.

Eventually, it was decided that smog must be banned. No one was allowed to burn anything but smokeless fuel in the cities. The soot and particles of other dirt which covered every building of any age in London were gradually cleaned off.

A different, more colourful city emerged.

At my secondary school, if smog was forecast, we were sent home much earlier than usual, so that we would be in before dark combined with smog made life a bit more dangerous still. Naturally, we were sorry when the smog ended. But perhaps we got a fuller education than if it had continued.

I didn't have any notion of pollution. I thought that we were being sent home early because it would be easier for kidnappers to pounce on us from the smog and spirit us away if it was dark as well.

Harrods sold smog masks made of scarlet satin, at the height of the panic.

My mother was a big fan of weather forecasts and set great store by what they predicted. Her large Victorian sun bonnet of faded blue cotton came out of the wardrobe for beach holidays; her "brolly" was always at the ready if rain seemed likely.

CHAPTER 19 – LOSS

When does childhood end? Is there a clearly defined moment or is it a long gradual process?

In 1957, when I was fourteen, a catastrophe took place in our family. My mother told me one morning, before school, that my cousin, Alastair, had been killed in a flying accident. His plane had taken off HMS Eagle in the Mediterranean and never returned. The wreckage was not found. A life so suddenly ended at the age of twenty-five shocked and appalled us all. She said, "I didn't tell you last night. It is easier to bear things when you hear them in the morning."

I went to school with my thoughts in chaos. How could someone die who was so young, intelligent, popular and full of life? Dying was for the old, wasn't it? I could hardly take it in. The cold war, fought out between Russia and the West all through the 1950s, was responsible. If we had not had to have servicemen and women permanently ready to fight another, perhaps nuclear, war Alastair would not have had to be taking off from an aircraft carrier and risking his life.

If we, in our family, were devastated, how much worse was it for his parents and siblings? "Those whom the gods love die young" was an idea which gripped me. There seemed to be too many instances of this.

My conviction, established after reading 'On the Beach' that we were unlikely to live our full life span because of the hovering threat of nuclear war, was reinforced by Alastair's death. The pessimism induced by the book and the loss lasted several years until it became clearer that there was a "balance of terror" between the great powers, in which neither side would start a major war.

Minor wars continued, of course.

With Alistair's own family, the repercussions were immense. Three years after his untimely death, his mother, Elizabeth, threw herself from a fourth-floor window and was found dead below. Ten years on, the next brother in the family, Andrew, also killed himself.

It was said that, because Andrew's mother had been an alcoholic since before he was born and because alcohol crosses the umbilical cord and affects the unborn baby, Andrew was in any case going to be a very different person from his brother, Alastair, and his sister, Lindsay. No doubt his mother's death and the manner of it, was a factor, as was Alastair's death.

The emotional fallout of these events was enormous. For me, Alastair's death was the breaking-up and destruction of my expectations about the future. Childish naiveté was replaced by an awakening; people could die young, people who couldn't face their lives any longer could end them and promising people could see no prospect of an end of their grief.

Alastair's death was the first traumatic event of my life. Wildly unexpected, the shock and pain were severe. With his death, I left childhood behind.

Later, when my cousin, Julian, also decided to end his life, the family which had contained twelve first cousins was reduced to nine. Two of the three uncles on my mother's side were now bereaved parents, dazed by loss.

Julian's reasons for choosing to die were different. He'd been evacuated to America for the war years and been away from parental care for some time. He'd become a trainee film producer and worked with Carol Reed. He fell in love with Prunella Scales. She wouldn't marry him, so he took an overdose. The family was reeling. The family's wound was my wound, and my sisters'.

A pall of depression lay over the family following these deaths. For the parents of the three young men, it must have been a pall of anguish. Of course, during the intervening and following years there were also births and successes. There were marriages, second marriages, promotions and the establishment of dynasties.

When I saw my Uncle Hugh for the last time, at the Priory Clinic where staff were trying to wean him off alcohol, a nurse said to me, out of my uncle's hearing, that he had never got over the death of his son. And no wonder.

CHAPTER 20 – REMARKABLE RELATIONS

My father had a younger brother, Charles, of whom we saw very little. When I was old enough to be curious, I asked why this was. I was told that he suffered from severe mental illness. Until I was much older, I couldn't grasp what this meant in terms of difficult relationships.

He had been a Major in the Thirteenth Frontier Force of Rifles of the Indian Army. When the Second World War broke out, he was taken prisoner. For some time, it was not known whether he was alive or dead. His mother wrote a poem, while still uncertain of his fate, expressing her anguish.

He endured several years of captivity in a German prison camp. When he was repatriated at the end of the war, he discovered that his wife had deserted him and gone off with another man. Such was the veil of secrecy drawn over this marriage that I never even knew her name.

As a result of these two traumatic experiences, his mental health, perhaps already affected by his parents' broken marriage, collapsed altogether.

For twenty years he lived only a few miles from us at Ruislip. I never saw him there. In 1967, unable to face his life any longer, he gassed himself. What can one say? None of my close relations was killed in that war, but his life was destroyed by it all the same. Born just before the First World War, his life was destroyed by the Second World War, just as surely as if he'd been killed in action.

I knew nothing of his talents or capacities. All that remains of him is the gravestone at Brookwood Military Cemetery, where he lies beneath the great forest trees, at peace after the turmoil of his life.

My father's sisters, who lived until 1994 and 95, were a big influence on us.

Aunt Jessie, who had a degree, was the most educated woman in my family. She had worked for many years as a research assistant at the Royal Marsden Hospital.

Her intellectual gifts found a number of outlets. She knew a lot of her family's history and could articulately explain its intricacies. As a dedicated Christian, she volunteered her help in organising a stewardship scheme, which necessitated many hours of voluntary labour. In the discussion of any question, she was able to make a clear analysis of the issues.

But there was not enough outlet for her emotional energies. She did not marry, although she came close to it with a clergyman. Her early experience of a broken home convinced her that it was better not to marry than to marry and risk unhappiness.

After work, she took the bus back to her flat each day. It had a big window overlooking allotments; beyond those was Fulham Palace itself and beyond that the Thames. Whenever I visited her, we watched the sunset over the trees of the palace. It was a view we were both deeply attached to.

She lived in this flat in a very austere way. Although the rent rose continually, she stayed on in it after retirement, although her capital could perhaps have bought her a home outside London. She never invested in anything as modern as a vacuum cleaner but remained devoted to her carpet sweeper.

She loved sewing. She would make incredibly perfect darns of curtains, skirts, summer dresses or tablecloths. All the cupboards of her flat were full of sewing things: bits of fabric, cotton reels, embroidery silks and patchwork started but not complete.

She had an impressive knowledge of London's museums and art galleries. If I needed to know what bus went to some obscure part of the capital, she would always know which one to take.

Her generosity was remarkable and self-denying. When one of my sisters had financial problems she lent her a large sum — and then made this into a gift.

Towards the end of her life, ill health compelled her to go into a nursing home. She hated this, was depressed and negative, was not glad to see visitors and wouldn't sleep in a bed or wear her clothes. She was unable to hold her head up, so it dropped on her neck like a dying flower.

In my childhood, she'd been pretty and gay in the old sense. In my maturity, she'd become exhausted by her combination of illnesses. Her death was a merciful release.

Auntie Jessie's meticulous recording of every sum spent was an example of the thoroughness she applied to every task.

On a holiday in Florence in 1964, a much-needed break from caring for her ninety-four-year-old mother, she made a list of expenditure on every last stamp, cup of tea and bus fare. Methodical and orderly, she once told me that she never just added up a column of figures, but did it again a second time to check that the total was correct.

War-time thriftiness meant that when organising her wardrobe, she saved every last suspender, tiny pieces of tape too short to do anything with, fragments of lace trimming, and minute pieces of fabric in case they would come in useful later on. Everything was neatly sorted into cardboard boxes, along with silk and cotton reels, odd buckles and buttons from clothes which finally wore out and had to be thrown away.

Aunt Joyce, born 1909, lived in Hampstead until the family moved to Paignton for the years of the First World War. Her father continued his work in London. In 1919, they all moved to Queen Anne Street, where

145

her father also had his consulting rooms. She and Jessie went to Queen's College in Harley Street.

On leaving school, she spent six months in Paris and then became an art student at the Royal Academy Schools. She won a silver medal and the Creswick prize for landscape painting. She passed the Diploma.

After this, she did some portrait painting and then started designing textiles. A drawing by her is in the National Portrait Gallery.

During the late 1930s, she trained with the Red Cross in-home nursing.

When the Second World War began, she left her job with Calico Printers and became a VAD first in Hounslow, and then at the Household Cavalry School in Windsor, as her war service.

After the war, she returned to textile design and lived in Smith Street, Chelsea. This was before the King's Road had been ruined with loud music spilling out of downmarket shops and hideous supermarkets. It was elegant, restrained and full of beautiful clothes and furniture.

She coped with the stress of her younger brother's suicide, her elder brother's stroke and her mother's death within a two-year period.

In 1968, she left central London for Wimbledon, living in a gem of a nineteenth century cottage with a garden still (2005) possessed of an almost rural charm.

Moving further west still, to Salisbury, she joined several organisations, especially the Friends of

Salisbury Cathedral. Here, £6 million had to be raised for repairs. She did her bit for this. She attended the Cathedral every Sunday evening and, after her death in 1994, her ashes were buried in the Cathedral Close.

A usually self-effacing and modest person, she gave an example of devotion to the family. Her great appreciation of colour and design was transmitted to her nieces.

They were precious aunts, giving us a loving extended family. By their thrift and frugality, they were able to leave us capital to enable us to do things they themselves had never done.

Through their devotion to causes, they both made a solid contribution to the life of the community. Their exemplary dedication to causes ensured that, as long as I and my sisters survived, they would never be forgotten.

As I examine and repair an exquisite piece of patchwork she did, I am impressed all over again by her unerring taste, her technical ability as a needlewoman and her brilliant selection of fabric designs of the 1930s.

These patches, small fragile emblems of a whole era of design lie there; patterns alternating with plain green, black, grey and purple. There are flower prints, checks, abstract designs and embroidered pieces, with one even printed with "Joyce" in lipstick red. The quilt as a whole represents her to me. Silk, rayon, cotton and moiré; she understood how each fabric should be used.

My father's mother was Florence Wansey, born 1870. She had married my grandfather, Ralph Thompson, but they had separated long before I was born.

Probably her Christian name was, like that of many of her female contemporaries, in honour of Florence Nightingale, the heroine of the Crimean War of 1854-57. By 1870, Miss Nightingale's achievements were well-known.

My grandfather lived a solitary existence in a hotel in London, my grandmother lived in a bungalow in Ruislip. My only memory of my grandfather is of his asking me, when old and stiff, to help him fasten his shoelace. When I couldn't do it the way he wanted me to, he was angry. His temper was famous at Guy's Hospital, where my father-in-law was a medical student at the time of my grandfather's consultant post there.

My grandfather had been in the Artists' Rifles in the First World War. He then became an anatomy demonstrator before being made a consultant urologist. He died when I was twelve, and there was a big funeral at Guy's Hospital.

My father's mother lived until I was twenty-one. She had been deaf all her life after having measles in her youth. In her house, I remember a colourful rag rug, a hand-made item of the kind people had before the era of fitted carpets everywhere. Quinces grew in the garden, a magic place with little paths between big shrubs.

Like my maternal grandmother, she was wretchedly afflicted with arthritis. Later, poor sight and increasing immobility made her virtually a prisoner in the flats where her two daughters cared for her when she was unable to manage on her own.

At ninety-five, when she was being looked after by two daughters already facing their own health problems, she died. I would like to have known her in her prime. She must have been a capable person, for she brought up four children, a lot of the time single-handedly.

In the last years of her life, I made a drawing of her, thinking to practise the principles I was being taught at art school. The resultant piece of work was a maze of lines and wrinkles. I hope it conveyed the suggestion of a person who had survived many tragedies.

As a young woman, she stares out of photographs taken in the 1890s, her hair piled up, her figure controlled by corsets, with a shy expression.

She showed great expertise in the domestic arts of knitting, crocheting and making jam, unfashionable today but recognised in her time as valuable attributes.

By the time I knew her, she was a tired old lady, much affected by her arthritic pain and inadequately treated deafness.

My mother had said, more than once, that if you had lived through two world wars, you were entitled to be tired. I felt pity for my grandmother, realising how awful it must be to be indoors all day, especially in beautiful weather, but I'm not sure if it was love. For love to exist, there has to be communication, and her deafness tragically prevented that.

The loss of her garden must have been particularly painful to her, as I later understood, having formed a great attachment to all the gardens I or my family tended.

On my mother's side of the family, I knew only my grandmother, known to all her grandchildren as Gan-Gan. Born in 1872, she had gone to the Slade and been taught by the great Henry Tonks. She married John Stewart Mackintosh and had five children, of whom my mother was the youngest, being born in 1910. My grandfather died just after my parents were married, so I never knew him.

Grandfather Mackintosh had an obituary both in the British Medical Journal and in The Times. A doctor of medicine, a member of the Royal College of Surgeons and a Licentiate of the Royal College of Physicians. His first practice was his only one. When he came to Platts Lane, Hampstead, in 1898, the area was still surrounded by fields. His practice grew as the district did and, when leukaemia forced him to retire in 1933, he had one of the largest practices in the area.

At Sandgate, Folkestone, he studied his own illness, and psychotherapy, a particular interest. His hobbies were anthropology and watercolour painting.

The pictures he painted on Romney Marsh show a pastoral world remote from his London existence. The level meadows, the distant blue ridge of the Downs, stooks of corn and grazing sheep suggest his enjoyment of the rural idyll. To his family, they are precious reminders of his remarkable embrace of what became known years later as the Two Cultures.

My three great aunts, sisters of John Stewart Mackintosh, were redoubtable figures. Flora, Katie and Elsie.

Gan-Gan was a portrait painter. In spite of having the five offspring, her talent developed to a professional standard. All her children were painted as children. The staff employed gave her sufficient free time to advance as a painter. Domestic workers were very cheap at the time.

The household was described to me by my mother as "plain living and high thinking." There were regular readings aloud of Shakespeare plays, in which my grandparents and their friends all took part. The typed cast lists which were circulated to members refer to "Miss", "Mrs,", "Dr Mackintosh" and "Mr" someone else. This was their preferred method of address and underlines the formality of manners in the period 1910-25.

Gan-Gan had commissions to paint other subjects too. One of her achievements was a Madonna and Child painted for Mowbray's, the old established religious art business. This was a circular painting of which reproductions were for sale.

Her scrapbook also records an appeal by Arthur Waugh, father of Evelyn and Alec, for funds to commemorate her presentation of a portrait of the Vicar of St. Judes, to the church. She did this work for nothing and asked for donations to be put into the church's building fund.

Gan-Gan was immensely influential to all her descendants. Because she lived until I was twenty-one, I was able to benefit from her insights for much longer than some grandchildren can. Her great level of skill as a painter, her fortitude, gentleness and generosity are vivid to me although it is fifty-six years since she died.

CHAPTER 21 – THE UNCLES AND THEN AND NOW

Twenty-first-century visitors to the Antarctic may be amused or amazed to read the equipment list issued to my late uncle, Neil Mackintosh.

He was one of the scientific staff aboard the Discovery expedition of 1924. He was expected not only to bring, but also to use, a dinner jacket, a pair of white kid gloves, two soft hats, five dress ties (three white, two black), one or two tweed jackets, a navy blue lounge suit, a Burberry or mackintosh, one dress suit, one white waistcoat, one peaked yachting cap, four dozen handkerchiefs, one dozen of these (it was decreed) blue or khaki, one pair of evening shoes, and eight evening shirts, four of them starched.

Two shirts of "white ducks" were deemed insufficient. There also had to be two shirts of "white mess ducks".

The clothes to be supplied by the government included a topee, fur mittens, balaclava helmets, overalls, oilskins, jumpers, sweaters, khaki shirts and Wolsey vests and pants.

Of course, the list also included rather more down-to-earth items like three pairs of warm pyjamas, two woollen mufflers — did they wear them both together, I wonder? — two strong braces, numerous spare buttons and the needles with which to sew them on, not forgetting the essential accessory for all travellers, a safety pin.

Notwithstanding this immense quantity and variety of outfits, those embarking were warned that "cabin space was extremely limited." Where on earth did he put it all?

"On the Discovery" the instructions continue, "Staff will dress for dinner when the ship is in port, but at sea, any old clothes of any kind may be worn."

The tradition of the British gentleman explorer was being firmly upheld; participants had to look smart and well-turned-out at any moment when other people might catch sight of them.

If only we could have known more; what books they took with them and how did they manage being herded together at very close quarters when on board? Did they tire of each other's company?

And how did people accustomed to the temperate climate of Britain adjust to the temperatures they were to encounter, not just fleetingly as cruise visitors might, but for the whole season?

Some additional insight into the organisation of the trip appears in the letters exchanged between my uncle and the Secretary of the Discovery Committee. On paper stamped "Colonial Office", an Edward Baynes "desired to inform" my uncle that it would not be necessary to list his qualifications a second time and was asked to say what experience he'd had of "sea voyages, handling boats, snow or ice conditions, ski-running, scientific work at sea, marine biology at coastal stations, or any other matters which might be useful to the expedition."

Four months later, in May 1924, my uncle was offered a temporary appointment as a zoologist on the scientific staff of the expedition, with a salary of £600 a year and "free messing or an allowance in lieu thereof."

He was sternly warned that the appointment was not pensionable. Perhaps that wasn't too worrying for someone who was still only twenty-three and, anyway, the contract was only for three years in the first instance.

Everything was conditional on passing the medical examination.

He was warned that he must not publish any of his findings relating to the expedition without the "instructions" of the Discovery Committee.

He was informed that the studies he was to pursue should be largely concerned with the reproduction of marine animals.

This letter came from Downing Street and was signed, "I am, Sir, your obedient servant, G. Grindle."

My uncle's handwritten reply in his neat legible script, accepting the appointment, is dated May 30th,

1924. The days of the word processor were far in the future.

The contract was renewed in 1927-28, and again in 1931-34.

Stanley Kemp sent a letter in 1927 warning my uncle not to refer to any "controversial matters anything which implies criticism of Government action", in a lecture which my uncle was due to give at Sheffield University.

The letter from Stanley Kemp dated 2nd December 1924 records that cables had been received at the Colonial Office recording my uncle's safe arrival in South Georgia.

"You will surely find a number of necessary things omitted; please send detailed lists of these as soon as possible." More opportunity for making long lists evidently.

It goes on "Wheeler has the key of the medicine chest." One hopes he never mislaid it.

The expedition was to be allowed £50 for coal, £25 for fresh meat and veg. from Montevideo and Stanley, and £10 for "incidentals". "I imagine the amounts will be ample for six months," he was told.

A final letter in the file, dated 1929, states that consideration had been given to payment of salaries to employees of the Discovery Committee, in the event of war breaking out. Salaries and benefits would continue to be paid between the outbreak of any hostilities and call-up into the forces. It is remarkable to read that ten years before the Second World War actually began, the more farsighted people were already realising the need to plan for it.

I remember Neil as an extremely modest man whose learning was lightly worn. He never monopolised the conversation or insisted on telling people with little scientific education about the world of marine biology. To us, he was a kind and generous figure. Being a bachelor, he left what funds he'd managed to accumulate to his nephews and nieces.

The lists and letters left behind after his death remind us of an era when upholding sartorial standards was as vital in the remote world of the Antarctic as it was back home.

Although he was a distinguished scientist, his interests were not confined to science. A reading of his will revealed that he had left a sum of money to the Handel Opera Society. In his full life, science alone was not enough.

The most startling reminder that the men of the expeditionary staff inhabited a different world is the pair of wooden skis, used in South Georgia, which have come down to us from my late uncle's possessions. They represent a wholly different technology from our own. With such primitive aids, my uncle and his colleagues achieved their objectives.

My mother's three brothers were all older than she was. Hugh, Kenneth and Neil were highly contrasted characters, and all had special qualities.

In their World War One uniforms, they look seriously out of a sepia photograph, faces youthful and unlined, so different from their appearance when I first knew them in the late 1940s and early 1950s.

My Uncle Hugh, who was born in May 1899, told me he felt fortunate to have survived a war in which so many of his friends and contemporaries were slaughtered. His conversations with me when I had reached adulthood revealed also feelings of guilt over being alive when they were dead.

He made a living from business but wrote an exacting form of poetry, the ballade, in his spare time. Four volumes sit on our bookshelves; the slenderness of each book ornamented with a repeat design markedly different from the surrounding novels and collected verse of full-time poets.

His university had been Neuchâtel, where he specialised in French and German. At Sherborne, his friend had been Alec Waugh, a novelist who became famous in the 1920s and 1930s. The Waugh family were also neighbours in Hampstead.

He had a prodigious memory and impressive linguistic skills, speaking five or six languages. Hilaire Belloc was also a friend, one who shared his literary interests.

He was famously attracted to women, and when I was an impressionable twenty-one, loftily announced to me that it was very good for marriages for the husband to have a discreet (heavily emphasised) mistress. He made no pronouncement as to his view of whether wives should have the same freedom — but this was 1964.

Despite Hugh's tendency to stray, my Aunt Winifred, a woman of great character, intelligence and kindness, remained married to him till he died. She was the daughter of an Argentinean millionaire. Her sister, Eileen Agar, was a surrealist artist who moved in august circles, and who had been the girlfriend of Paul Nash.

Hugh was said to have reacted against what he saw as the strict Puritanism of my great aunts, his aunts. After the slaughter and waste of his generation in the trenches, hedonism was a way of trying to forget that traumatic era.

Some of this he explained to me at a lunch at the Athenaeum when I was twenty-one. He'd taken me there as a birthday treat. I was amazed to be offered, in addition, a weighty copy of the Oxford Companion to English Literature. It has been my most faithful companion ever since. On the way back afterwards, he stopped the car, disappeared into a chemist, and came back with a bottle of scent for me.

He'd been considered something of an expert on the export of goods to South America. In 1941, he gave a talk on the radio about economic conditions in Latin America. My grandmother preserved the text in her scrapbook.

My recall of him at his very best was when my parents and I were having a meal with him and Winifred at his flat in Chelsea. I don't remember how the subject came up, but all at once he was quoting, in full and word-perfect, Keats' Ode on Melancholy. It was completely spellbinding. He had reached an age when old men forget but had not forgotten.

In old age, his decline was sad. I visited him at a drying-out clinic. He told me how badly he needed a drink. One of the nurses told me, out of his hearing, that he had been unable to recover from the death of his only son. And no wonder.

Not long afterwards, he broke a thigh in a fall and had to be operated on to set the bone. He did not survive the operation.

Of my three Mackintosh uncles, it was Kenneth who had the most dramatic entry into the world.

He was born with a condition called congenital hypertrophic stenosis of the pylorus. Until the time of his birth, it was always fatal before the age of three or four months. He was not expected to live. However, having been born into a medical family, he was operated on on the kitchen table at Corner House, survived and thrived.

Later in life, he served in both the First and Second World Wars, played rugby for the London Scottish, played polo when stationed on Malta, became Naval Attaché at the British Embassy in Paris and finally, Yeoman Usher to Black Rod in the House of Lords. He was honoured by having a KCVO conferred on him — a distinction in the personal gift of the Queen.

The success of the operation (in 1902) on this tiny baby was written up in medical magazines and carefully preserved by my grandmother. In the articles about this, the contrasting fate of other babies born with the same problem was described. These infants had been unlucky enough to be born before the new operation to save them had been devised.

The history of his treatment was conveyed to us as children; being so ignorant of medicine, the part which most impressed me was that the kitchen table had been the setting of this miracle — the everyday mixed with the sensational. The realm of the cook had briefly become the realm of the surgeon.

In our drawing room stands a low round table with a brass edge. Its battered surface shows many scratches. These reveal the table's purpose in the earlier decades of the twentieth century; Kenneth let off fireworks from it in the garden of Corner House.

The fireworks symbolised, perhaps, some aspects of his own life and of the times through which he lived. Although damaged, the table survives in our house. Although damaged, he survived to seventy-six, and in our memories now.

An account of these losses appears in Chapter 19. Kenneth was sent to Dartmouth Naval College at the age of twelve. This establishment, a tough and strict one, was intended to produce naval officers. Instant obedience to orders, respect for the naval hierarchy and knowledge of naval tradition, navigation and all other lore of the sea were his daily fare.

As a midshipman, the most junior grade, he emerged straight into the First World War. He, fortunately, survived this and proceeded up the naval career ladder. In 1926, he married Elizabeth Fawcett, whose father was an officer in the Indian Army.

In the Second World War, he captained ships on the Artic Convoy run.

My memory is of a much-travelled man with wide experience of several different kinds of life. He was at ease in any company. When I was fifteen, he asked me to go with him on a day trip to France held for the cleaners and caretakers at the House of Lords. He was just as much at home in their company as with that of the peers who sat in the House. He had been appointed Yeoman Usher to Black Rod in the House of Lords.

He also wrote extremely good letters; brief, succinctly expressed and sent promptly in thanks for lunch or in reply to other letters. His romantic nature also surfaced in these. In terms of devotion to duty and courage in facing an exceptional series of losses, he could not be faulted. An account of these losses appears in my final chapter. As a role model, I found him near-perfect.

His retirement from the House of Lords in December 1970 was marked by two-and-a-quarter pages of tributes to him in the House and recorded in

Hansard. Speeches were made from all parts of the House praising his work.

My recollection of his funeral, forty-three years ago now, was that the passage was read which relates particularly to naval people: "They that go down to the seas in ships and have their business in great waters; these men see the works of the Lord, and His wonders in the deep."

But when I consulted the service sheet for his funeral, I found I was wrong. Instead, the great passage from the Wisdom of Solomon was read which starts, "But the souls of the righteous are in the hands of God and no torment shall touch them." By contrast, the service ended with the playing of 'Every nice girl loves a sailor'.

He had fought to defend his country and went on to serve it in other ways. He had founded and loved a family of his own, and had continued to function brilliantly as son, brother, uncle and friend.

For me, the image of Kenneth which stays with me is the photograph of him now in the possession of his great-nephew, Jonathan Davies. It shows him walking purposefully in full captain's uniform along the deck of his ship. Beside him is another figure, instantly recognisable not just to me but to the whole Western World. It is Winston Churchill. During that time they conversed together, a member of our family was seen with a person of world-class power and influence, in their common task of defeating the enemy.

My mother's third brother was Neil. An immensely kind, shy and retiring man, he became a distinguished scientist. At Imperial College, he showed an aptitude for zoological research and in the two years after graduation produced two papers on the crystalline style of gastropods and the chrondo cranium of fish (1923).

He was at the beginning of the great enterprise The Discovery Investigations of the Antarctic Seas. In 1924 he led the advance party to establish and take charge of the Marine Laboratory for the study of whales in South Georgia. Later he took part in three major expeditions of the 'Discovery II', being leader of two circumpolar voyages and bringing back a wealth of information about plankton.

In 1936 he became Director of Research, until 1949 when the Investigations were merged with the new National Institute of Oceanography, of which he became Deputy Director.

His contributions to knowledge lay in two main fields: the biology and conservation of whales, and the oceanic macroplankton.

As my uncle, and as a childless bachelor, he left to each of his nieces and nephews an equal legacy of about £4000. This enabled us to put down a deposit on our house, for which I will ever be grateful. I was still a child when he was awarded a CBE and didn't realise what a distinction this was. A lifelong smoker, he only reached the age of seventy-three. I went to his Golders

Green funeral with my red-haired four-year-old and one- year old, his great-nephews.

CHAPTER 22 – ATTITUDES and DISCIPLINE

When I demanded attention for my needs or problems and became a complete nuisance doing so, my father would announce magisterially, "Judith, you are not the only pebble on the beach".

Of all the thousands of things people have said to me in my lifetime, that is one of the few dozen never forgotten.

From my mother, I absorbed that attitude in which every single object in the house which had belonged to an ancestor was invested with special qualities. For that reason, and because the emotions attached to that now-dead relation were now attached to the object, it was very difficult to dispose of something.

Indeed, many of these objects possessed other qualities than merely having been the property of an ancestor; they were beautiful. Some of them were functional as well.

All our lives with our parents, my mother warned us to be very careful in the vicinity of antiques, as they could so easily be broken. "No horseplay," she would say firmly, as we surged around letting off steam.

Later, as many of these objects, despite their fragility, were still around long after my parents and sister had died, I realised that actually these things last quite well. It is people who don't. Whose lives are of such brief duration, whose bodies are less robust than porcelain, glass or mahogany.

My mother also kept carefully every single school report all three of us had ever received and every letter we'd sent our parents while away from home. My mother even kept all the letters she'd written to her parents while visiting South Africa in 1931.

An attitude passed on to us with great emphasis was that we not only had to be grateful to relations when they gave us things or took an interest in us, but we also had to be grateful that we had any relations at all because there seemed to be so many people in the world who had none.

Our ironing lady, Miss Long, the only child of long-dead parents, never married and without children, was one such. As so often in such cases, we were her only family, the only young in whom she could take an interest.

At prayers at my secondary school, we were frequently told that much was expected from those to whom much is given. This idea, perhaps the most enduring of all the ideas I encountered there became, like St. Bennet's rule, something not forgotten. Not always lived up to, of course, but not forgotten.

Some core principles of my upbringing are easy to remember. The first was duty. You had a duty to take some notice of what school teachers said and you were supposed to do the same with what your parents said. In practice, perhaps you didn't accept that their advice had been valid till you looked back on it at the age of forty.

But you wore the marks of their influence; you didn't produce illegitimate offspring and you behaved with adequate respect to relations.

Duty meant that, as soon as Christmas was over, we had to write thank-you letters. To begin with, we lacked inspiration for these and appealed to our mother for suitable sentences to express our feelings.

In time, because we were expected to persist with this, we became of course much better at it. Later, when it became necessary to write much more difficult letters, including letters of condolence, we'd had the practice to make these possible.

It was made clear to us that if there were elderly, housebound or ill relations, there was a duty to visit them as often as practicable, and for however much time it took. It was true that most of our close relations were in southeast England, but within that space were many long distances. My parents did their duty by their very old, disabled mothers, who both lived into their nineties. The great aunts in Sussex were an awkward journey away, but they found the time to go there whenever they could.

The message was clear; you took care of relations in their old age.

Self-sacrifice was admired. We knew of people, and my great aunt, Elsie, was one, who had spent their entire lives caring firstly for ageing parents, then uncles or aunts, then sisters. Unless they gained satisfaction from this loving sacrifice, their lives were unfulfilled as neither marriage, children, career nor grandchildren came their way.

These women could find no husbands after the carnage of the First World War. Or they put the needs of others before their own need for fulfilment. Now, they are called "carers" and get a little, but probably not enough, recognition.

An important belief of my parents was that one had to be inconspicuous. One must not stand out in any way; good taste forbade it. One must never, by one's behaviour or appearance, excite critical comment. One must never, never "draw attention to oneself". The worst thing of all was to "make an exhibition of yourself". This expression was used on occasions when one of the three of us had had a public display of emotion or rebellion.

As far as discipline went if we behaved really badly, we were sent to our rooms. This was a surprisingly modern punishment in the late 1940s when corporal punishment was not only perfectly legal in schools of all kinds, but also actually approved of by many, especially for boys.

I was fearful of total rejection by my parents. One day, I was out with my mother in Harrow and we passed a door labelled "Child Guidance Clinic". I asked her what this meant. She said it was for children who were out of their parents' control. Was this me? I anguished over it.

There were a great many critical references to my behaviour at home.

When I was seven, I remember thinking despondently that I would have to have improved by the time I was twice my current age, or to what depths would my life have descended?

Was I worse than anyone else of my age? Or just worse than either of my sisters? At any rate, I was never sent to the Child Guidance Clinic.

My ignorance and lack of experience made me unable to judge my position in the moral universe.

Probably today it would be thought that our upbringing had been too sheltered.

At one time in my growing-up years, we were told not to walk down Grove Hill alone. This was one of several routes which led from the hilltop down to the main part of Harrow. On one side were detached houses, on the other a small wood.

From one of my better-informed friends, I discovered the reason for this ban. A man had been seen standing under the trees exposing himself. I don't think I ever heard he had attacked anyone; such people seem usually only to display and watch the reaction. But it wasn't thought proper in my family that we should know why there was a ban.

The ways of the world did intrude gradually into the protective shell of our upbringing. Near our house was an old cottage with an unusually fine, and lovingly tended garden. One day, we heard that the occupant, a single woman, had thrown herself onto the railway line in front of a train, after an unhappy love affair. What was love that people would die for it?

I had lingered to smell and admire the roses which cascaded over her garden wall. And now she would never again go to smell them herself.

She had been a gardener of distinction. How appropriate that her first name had been Violet.

Once adolescent, it was made clear we must not "throw ourselves" at a boy. This would be "making ourselves cheap". The concept of a "jeune fille", protected from worldly knowledge and experience was the aim impossible of achievement.

Nevertheless, I was seventeen, before I heard a four-letter word. When I did hear one, it was from the lips of a boy from Alleyn's School, Dulwich, who was a co-member of an archaeological dig I went on at Verulamium in 1960.

There was one exception to this seventeen year stretch of time. My father, when provoked to exasperation watching boys making mistakes on the rugger field would growl, "Silly arse!" In my ignorance,

171

I thought he was saying, "Silly ass," and that this was some odd way of pronouncing the word.

It was believed that by sending us to girls-only schools, we would be protected from contact with boys and therefore be able to concentrate on our work. I have to say there is some statistical support for this point of view. But one of the results was, on the part of some girls, an absolute obsession with men.

Our domestic science room at my secondary school overlooked the construction site of the new swimming pool. Builders of Greek, athletic build adorned it. One girl in my class found them of greater interest than learning to stitch a gingham apron.

CHAPTER 23 – DISCOVERING ART

I have mentioned the Friday afternoon art lessons at my first school as being the time of the week I most longed for.

But it was a brief exchange with my mother when I was eight which did the most to send me towards the way I chose to earn my living.

One evening, she fetched me from a party after dark. The car was not used for such expeditions then but was kept for major excursions. I was fetched on foot.

As we walked along the High Street towards Bradbys, I caught sight of the bare twigs and branches of a bush, silhouetted against the yellow light on a neighbour's porch. I told my mother it looked like lace.

"I'm so glad you notice things like that", she said. From noticing things like that, it was only a short step to wanting to paint them.

From painting them and talking about them, it was only a short step to enthusing others about the visual world and becoming an art teacher.

We also came from a home where it was normal to discuss the exact difference between two similar-looking colours. With a portrait-painting grandmother, a designer aunt, another miniature-painting aunt and a third aunt who, although engaged in scientific research, had an unusually well-developed appreciation of art, we lived surrounded by pictures and designs.

Down in Greater Harrow, where the long parades of shops were, was a large stationer which sold a wide variety of stuff. But the only goods which interested me were the marvellous paint boxes, ranging from pricey wooden ones with dozens of tubes right down to starter kits with just a few. I coveted these, and took every opportunity when in the shop, to open the many flat drawers in the display cabinets which contained individually wrapped, water-colour pans in those glowing, pure colours. If the window contained a range of materials, I would gaze into it, wistfully desiring to possess as much as I possibly could.

I was lucky in my father. He realised materials cost rather a lot and I could not finance them from my pocket money. He gave me some extra money so that I could paint. Considering how little he was paid (£1,700 a year was the most he ever earned), this was extremely generous.

He did something else for me which was very important. He asked his colleague who taught art at Harrow if I could come in for an hour or so on Saturday mornings.

There was a big late-Victorian Art School, an enormous space with a high ceiling, full of painting equipment, and an attached exhibition space, where pupils could study the work of different painters.

I loved the orderliness of this space; the boxes where coloured pencils, all sorted according to their colour, neatly sharpened, awaited use. I loved the still-lives set up for the boys to paint, the professional-looking easels and the special lectures given by visiting experts.

Here I had the opportunity, not only to learn a bit more about drawing and painting but also to look at the work of people considerably older than me.

The presiding genius was Maurice Percival. He only had one arm; the other had been damaged and removed in the war. I think he was the first person I knew to be able to do such an exacting job while suffering a serious disability. He never showed any awkwardness in moving furniture or arranging the studio as he wanted it. He was my first lesson in triumph over adversity, managing with one arm, a job few could manage with two.

He showed me how to do various things in art, but his value to me wasn't only about technique, or only about doing a job well when seriously handicapped. He reinforced my belief that art was a worthwhile human activity and that it had value. Not, of course, in a financial sense, but in that art and artists mattered as much as science and scientists, and as much as any other field of endeavour.

When I was considered old enough to travel alone into London on the tube, I went very often on Saturday mornings to draw historic costumes at the Victoria and Albert Museum. I never penetrated much further than the costume court, where big glass cases held all manner of farthingales, dresses with ruffs, crinolines, bustles and all the rest of the panoply of garments with which women had clothed themselves over the centuries.

The subtleties of embroidery, pattern design and colour eluded me completely. I found I couldn't get the proportions right, because I still hadn't learned how to do a measured drawing. The wealth of detail and decoration could only be conveyed in a very approximate way. But it was a passionate interest for a while.

Walking through South Kensington, one had to pass another very seductive art shop, with even more expensive and recherché equipment. So I had my weekly gaze into the windows there.

These expeditions introduced me to several ideas: that clothes could be an art form, that it was a miracle such fragile items had survived the upheavals, wars, moths and damp of two centuries or so and that museums were treasure houses.

To return to my mother's remark, "I'm so glad you notice things like that". The right remark at the right time. Most people can identify comments or statements made to them which, although the speaker may have forgotten them immediately, were remembered all their lives by the hearer.

Why did I remember what she said that day when so much else has been forgotten? I remembered it because it mattered to me.

The development of self-esteem wasn't, in those days, given the prominent place in child rearing that it has today. But at a crucial moment, my mother showed she did understand its importance. Later, when illness and tiredness had taken their toll, she was more negative about our ideas and schemes.

Our art materials were quite different from today. Every preschool and primary-age child in the twenty-first-century has a set of six brilliantly coloured felt pens, which they wield expertly.

We never had these. Poster colours in primary colours, in small jars we did have, and "paintboxes": cheap pigments with unsatisfactory colouring power. If we were lucky, we might be given a proper set of watercolours. But I was exceptionally lucky. Gan-Gan, my mother's mother, had become extremely arthritic by the mid-1950s. She had to give up oil painting as her fingers had become too stiff. One day, she presented me with a battered-looking, but solid, wooden oil painting box.

Its inside was lined with tin trays and there were several still usable large and small tubes of artists' oil paint in it. Some of the paints were in colours no longer made and some were so hard they had to be thrown away. But that paintbox sent one off on creative adventures I might never have had if that gift had not been made to me.

The box is a treasured object, being not just a container for materials. It represents the link between myself and my grandmother and a shared devotion to painting.

CHAPTER 24 – SIN and GUILT

Despite having moral ideas pumped into us at home, school and Sunday School, I sinned by both commission and omission.

I had a friend the same age as I was, whom I will call Jane. She came from a prosperous family and lived in a large-scale neo-Georgian villa, with an immense garden. This had an enviable quota of terraces, lawns and herbaceous borders.

She had a range of toys and other possessions whose quantity and variety aroused my envy. Her dolls' clothes, especially made me jealous. Her set of seventy-two Derwent coloured pencils was something I longed for, had never had and never would have. She wasn't particularly interested in drawing and colouring pictures, as I was, and was quite casual about her ownership of them.

One day while playing at her house, temptation overcame me. I stole one of her dolls' dresses and took it home. How did it all end? Conveniently, perhaps, I forget. Did my mother demand to know where I had got it from? It is now too late to ask. Maybe it was tearfully given back. Maybe it was concealed forever, out of shame. I knew perfectly well this was wrong behaviour.

Jane's parties were legendary. Every year, her parents threw a spectacular firework party. There were lavish amounts of fireworks, a bonfire, on which every piece of waste wood had been piled for months past, and a fat stuffed Guy Fawkes on top.

The flames were encouraged by cans of petrol being chucked at the bonfire. What can it all have cost? As the last firework showered golden rain and there were only embers left in the bonfire, we were led indoors to an enormous appetising spread laid out in the dining room. Someone (was it me?) started throwing food under the table and laughing. I certainly joined in, and for years afterwards was ashamed at taking part.

It was in this house, I think, where I first started to believe that being well-off would be nice. The family who lived here also had a second home — a cottage at West Wittering where, despite my awful behaviour, I was invited to stay in the summer holidays.

After we were eleven, we stopped seeing anything of each other. Jane was sent to a boarding school, I to a day school. We lost touch.

So, I was covetous, greedy and selfish.

CHAPTER 25 – SEX

A local doctor's daughter, one of three girls, as we were, showed me one of her dolls, dressed in some rather bulky clothes. They were probably hand-knitted, just as most babies' clothes were in those days. She told me the doll looked as though she was pregnant.

I asked what that meant — I suppose we were both about nine at the time. "Don't you know what pregnant means?" she asked incredulously. I felt foolish. She told me. The word was common currency in her house; it had never been uttered in ours.

What did we know? Nothing beyond the biological facts, and then only at eleven. The commonplace events in the lives of today's adolescents: oral sex in dark parks, pregnancies instead of exams at 11+ and 15+, and STDs in ever-mounting numbers were almost unheard of. I knew a couple of girls who were made pregnant while at school — but only a couple, out of one hundred girls in the lower sixth and upper sixth.

Were we any worse off for our innocence? I don't think we were. Sexual intercourse was not regarded as a right which anyone acquired by simply taking a girl out on one occasion.

Unlike the two generations which preceded my own, we were allowed to know the facts of life, and that was useful knowledge. Because we went, at secondary level, to all-girls schools, we didn't have that daily contact with boys which enabled us to feel at ease with them. We entered adulthood in a state of inexperience which would be regarded as extraordinary today.

There was a divide, though, between the people we were by day, clad in a uniform intended to conceal whatever attractiveness we might have had, and the people we were at evenings and weekends.

At those times, we were just as desperate to look seductive as any factory worker, student or secretary.

At the age of eleven or twelve, I began to realise something was missing from my life. It didn't take long to discover that this missing thing was love, not the love I assumed I was receiving from my parents and the extended family, but love from a boy. The yearning to have this lasted years, through several passionate infatuations, almost always on my part, but once on the part of a boy I knew. Eventually, I realised this was a perfectly normal need.

No one among my contemporaries talked about gay relationships, although these must have existed. It was regarded as very usual, at my secondary school, to have a "crush" on sixth-form girls. We grew out of this heroine worship. Today, it might be said that these cool, sophisticated people of 17+ were our role models. In

182

comparison with them, we were grubby, inarticulate and often plain or spotty.

But we weren't immune to heartbreak. Hearing that someone I admired very much, from a distance, had asked out a girlfriend of mine was as painful for me as for anyone of any generation. I spent quite a few of my teenage years crying myself to sleep because of rejection.

The agony and the ecstasy; more of the former than the latter for me. I tended to confuse attraction with love. To be "in love" with someone who felt the same about oneself, seemed a more important and pressing ambition than anything to do with careers, marriage or being famous. Wanting to be loved became an overriding need.

Ahead lay falling in love to the sound of Henry Mancini's "Moon River". Those moments when one suddenly realised the strength of one's feelings for someone; I thought they were the supremest happiness. Later, as a parent myself, I discovered the equal or greater happiness of realising one's love for children.

Were we overly influenced by childhood fairy stories of falling in love and being happy ever after? Probably we were. Romance was all, and when I discovered E.M. Forster's saying that, "Romance was a figure with outstretched arms yearning for the unattainable," I recognised a profound truth.

CHAPTER 26 – VANISHING COUNTRYSIDE

When we were children, no one got excited or angry if, on a country walk, we picked a bunch of wildflowers. It was seen as a normal thing to do. It was regarded as a mark of appreciation for their shape, colour, smell and charm if one arrived home with a few stems to put in water.

The experience of performing this simple act, of wanting to possess part of what had been seen and enjoyed in the country, was extremely formative in my life.

From it, I learned to love flowers born wild and cultivated, and from that, gardening and all kinds of growing, indoors and out.

Now, those uncomplicated and spontaneous acts are illegal. No matter how commonplace a plant is, one must not pick it. Even such abundant flowers as cadmium-yellow ragwort, burnt sienna sorrel, mauve knapweed and primrose yellow honeysuckle growing in such profusion near my home, are protected. It is regarded as wrong to pick them. Something which in my early life was both educational and pleasurable is now forbidden.

Of course, legislators would say that if everyone today picked all the wildflowers they wanted, there would be none left. That may well be true. The population in my childhood was so much smaller, so pressure on the countryside was so much less.

In 1951, when I was eight, the census said that there were 50.2 million in Britain. Of course, there were fewer vehicles, less crowded roads and fewer visits to the countryside.

There are fewer birds of some species as I write this, because of the intensive farming methods and widespread use of agrochemicals. To me, the saddest loss is the butterflies. In good summers like 2003, there seemed to be a lot, but when I was a child, there were always many more than now.

My cousin, Moray Mackintosh, whose country childhood home had been in a village near Horsham, told me that when he used to go out into the field behind the cottage, clouds of butterflies had fluttered around him. That was in the early 1950s. You would not find that in 2023.

I remember in the early 60s going with my father by car from Harrow to Oxford, via Fingest in the Chilterns. In one of the fields we passed, there was a sea of cowslips in full flower. In the twenty-first century, the only places I have seen these growing are on motorway embankments, where they can flourish unpicked.

My mother deplored the hacking down of hedgerows, especially in East Anglia, to make bigger fields more efficient at producing food.

Once, to protect a tree which workmen were about to cut down for no apparent reason, she prevented its loss simply by demanding an explanation from the workmen's employer.

When we were children, there was still undeveloped land, with a patch of blackberry bushes yielding large succulent fruit, at the top of Sudbury Court Drive.

Now, where that once was, there are roomy detached houses for the prosperous commuter, with neat gardens. The country has been driven further back. Will there be any left for our children's grandchildren?

I remember my mother's anguish when, in 1956, a huge, magnificent beech tree in the garden of the house opposite the park, had to be cut down.

We became conservationists by both nature and nurture. With my mother's stout defence of the whole natural world, it was impossible that we should have become anything else.

CHAPTER 27 – HOW THE WAR AFFECTED MY GENERATION

Many of my contemporaries had little or no contact with their fathers between birth and six years old because these fathers were away at the war. No doubt children of both sexes missed this vital contact with fathers, but boys lacked a role model, so possibly it was a more serious lack for them. Other children, born in the 1930s, reached adolescence without the presence of a father they remembered from early childhood and had to get to know him again as teenagers.

But there were worse effects of the war than the absent father who eventually returns. The father of one of our contemporaries had been killed in the war. Another lost his father very early on as a result of war wounds. There were thousands of war widows and children whose fathers would never come home.

Did the fact that our father was absent for much of the war make us more anxious than children born later? Did we absorb from our mother her anxiety about whether everybody in the family would survive the war?

Some children were no doubt affected in this way. In 1940, while the Battle of Britain raged over southeast

England, my mother had to decide, when the air-raid siren sounded, whether to go down to the air-raid shelter first and then feed the baby or feed the baby first and then go. Were those anxieties transmitted to the baby herself?

Some children were affected in this way. But communities were stronger units than they are now. The sense of "all being in this together" which prevailed during the war seemed to last after VE Day and unite people of different views. The solidarity of society against a common enemy may have helped to offset the disadvantages created by the war.

The phenomenon called evacuation was highly developed by 1940. Some of those sent away suffered psychological damage from being separated from their parents at too young an age, others suffered at the hands of unwelcoming host families.

In the first big wave of evacuation, my mother with her small new first baby, Joanna, did not take part. The baby was only a few months old and she and my mother stayed in Harrow.

When the flying bombs (pilotless aircraft) started in 1944, things were different. Joanna, then four, I aged seventeen months, and our mother were invited to stay with friends in Norfolk until the terror subsided. The London area was regarded as quite dangerous.

These friends had an old mill house. Away from the risks of staying in Harrow, it was believed that we would survive the war. By being with one parent, we had the reassurance of her presence. The photographs show Joanna happily adapting to country life. We had a debt of gratitude to these people who gave us a safe haven which could never be repaid.

We were fortunate in that our parents had taken thought of our safety, and in that, an offer of hospitality came from friends. Dreadful incidents of mass slaughter in London came gradually to my notice in the years following the war. Many victims were children. More than seven thousand seven hundred children were killed by enemy action in Britain.

Rationing made little sense to children. The only aspect of it I remember was sweet-rationing. Looking at it now from a very different perspective, there could be few things more helpful to the nation's health than the reduction of the amount of sugar and fat consumed.

The ending of rationing, which had been applied to clothes as well as food, did not end the hoarding instinct, because it had been virtually impossible to obtain anything during the period 1939-45, so people hung on to all sorts of objects which in times of peace and plenty would have been thrown away. Broken and redundant furniture, shrunk and worn clothes, chipped crockery, very short pieces of string; these might all have a future use and therefore were kept.

Garages, lofts and attics filled up. My sister, Joanna, was heavily influenced by this need to keep things which could have been disposed of.

I became a scavenger. On walks, I collected fir cones for firelighters, sloes for gin, driftwood cast up by the sea for fuel and plant cuttings from derelict gardens. It all reached a climax when I found some unwanted windows in a skip and Hugh, my husband, incorporated them into his new shed.

People became adept at making clothes from unexpected materials. Not long ago, The Times carried letters celebrating nightdresses and wedding dresses made from parachute silk. This resourcefulness became a feature of the national character and was still in evidence decades later.

The fact that not much could be bought meant a great emphasis on growing one's own food, making or mending one's own clothes and making things last rather than acquiring new ones.

These were valuable ideas. From them came my lifelong pleasure in growing things and making them. The jug of flowers on the window-ledge, the desk my husband built of pine, the rag rugs and patchwork, the loaves of bread free of additives and the table my eldest son made at school are all valued pieces of the mosaic which is our life today.

During the 1940s and 1950s, a description one heard very often was "pre-war". Anything made before 1939 was assumed to be of better quality than anything made in any subsequent year.

If somebody came across, in a forgotten drawer or cupboard, a dress length of pre-war material, there were cries of delight. The lucky possessor was regarded with envy. The discovery of such an emblem of pre-war plenty was a subject for discussion and reflection.

I think we were also led to believe in a world of pre-war standards in behaviour and morals. The world of the 1920s and 1930s was seen, by the 1950s, through rose-coloured glasses, its poverty and unemployment were conveniently overlooked.

We had seen London knocked about by war. We knew of people who had died in that war. We knew that what had happened once could happen again. Did our insecurity come from this knowledge?

Because of wartime rationing, we'd been influenced by parents who had had to become very careful of resources of all kinds, especially food. So we knew waste was wrong and so was greed. We knew leftovers had to be used up, that bones must be boiled for soup and that clothes out-grown by cousins and friends must be used until finally worn out.

Did this make us too conscious of the value of material things? Or perhaps it made us sensible people who knew that there was only a finite supply of anything.

The war left its physical traces on the landscape of England. The countryside had altered by more than the flat concrete "pillboxes" built beside beaches and canals and the lines of monolithic tank traps on the beaches.

All over East Anglia and Lincolnshire were former airfields from which the bombers had departed. Traces of old concrete remained in these flatlands. One I saw in Norfolk had since become a poultry farm. The land would have needed little in the way of levelling. Hurriedly converted for wartime use, what lingers on reminds us of the many young lives lost.

One-storey army camps also disfigured the country. Their corrugated iron and plain brick exteriors are still to be seen, derelict and sad decades later. Were they perhaps being kept for future use? Prisoner-of-war camps were used to house competitors in the 1948 Olympic Games, held in Britain.

Gun emplacements still litter the cliff walks outside Milford Haven. At Orfordness, weird structures from secret experiments stand like sculptures amid the wildflowers and pebbles.

Village and town war memorials put up after the First World War, had new names carved upon them.

Like the traces of mediaeval farming still visible in many of Britain's fields, the archaeological evidence of the Second World War is scattered in many locations and is still being unearthed. As I write, two thousand-pound bombs have been discovered and made safe.

So, the countryside we knew as children was subtly different from the one our parents had known in their childhood. Church spires, like the one at Yelverton, were removed so that planes could land and take off safely.

Some citizens were expected to make appalling sacrifices for their country.

Gunby Hall, a magnificent house built in 1700, was nearly demolished in order to build an airfield for wartime use. When the Montgomery-Massingberd who owned it was informed that this was about to happen, he made strenuous efforts to save it, all fruitless. As a final attempt, he appealed to King George VI. The building and its garden were not demolished. The runway was aligned in a different direction.

The waves of refugees which reached Britain during the 1930s meant that the society in which I grew up was much more cosmopolitan than the one my parents knew.

Society was immeasurably enriched by this influx of people, many of them Jewish and fleeing from Hitler. My secondary school had numerous pupils with German surnames, the children of these refugees. They were enviably intelligent and talented and usually more articulate and mature than their English peers.

The upheavals in Europe which culminated in the Second World War benefited my generation in one important respect; we mixed every day with people whose cultural origins were different from our own.

So much about this place, Harrow, from which we came, shaped our lives. But later, after marrying, I lived for over three years without a telephone in a flat over a stable in the middle of Warwickshire. The isolation of this life enabled me to value the contrasting one of living in a community.

Going back to Harrow years after having left it for good, was a mixture of intense emotion and shock that so much change had taken place.

My sisters and I no longer belonged to Harrow, but we were unmistakably its children.

CHAPTER 28 – PHOTO ALBUM

Childhood Games - Joanna on the right, Gillian in the middle and Judith on the left about 1948.

The family camping in Suffolk - summer 1954.

The instantly identifiable 1926 Rolls Royce owned by
my father about 1950.

- J. W. Thompson, Helen Thompson, Joanna and
Gillian Thompson and Shelia Gregory about 1953.

J.W. and Helen Thompson about 1953.

The hall and dining room at Bradbys in the 1950s.

The Park Lake where we took many walks in the 1950s.

Major J.W. Thompson - Harrow House Group 1955.

Bradbys, the Harrow boys' house the Thompson
family lived in, about 1955.

Judith at Les Andelys in about 1960.